MAKING SPACE

FOR PRESCHOOL MAKERSPACES

Robin Marx-Mackerley, MS
Teresa A. Byington, PhD
Sarah E. Wright, MEd
Cathryn L. Peshlakai, MEd

Photography by:
Robin Marx-Mackerley, Erin Skaggs,
Cathryn Peshlakai, Charlee Wright, Sarah Wright

Gryphon House
www.gryphonhouse.com

⚙️⚙️ DEDICATION ⚙️⚙️

To all of the amazing early childhood programs that let us be part of their creation of a makerspace.

Copyright

Bulk Purchase

Gryphon House books are available for special premiums and sales promotions as well as for fund-raising use. Special editions or book excerpts also can be created to specifications. For details, call 800.638.0928.

Disclaimer

Gryphon House, Inc., cannot be held responsible for damage, mishap, or injury incurred during the use of or because of activities in this book. Appropriate and reasonable caution and adult supervision of children involved in activities and corresponding to the age and capability of each child involved are recommended at all times. Do not leave children unattended at any time. Observe safety and caution at all times.

TABLE OF CONTENTS

 **PREFACE**

Several years ago, Robin (lead author) was preparing for a state early childhood conference, and she came across the term *makerspace*. She had never heard of the term, so she did some research on the topic. As she searched the internet, Robin found multiple definitions and ideas about different types of makerspaces; however, she did not find anything on the subject as it relates to early childhood programs. Robin made inquiries on her favorite social-media outlets. She asked if others had heard of the term *makerspace*, and most of the replies were along the lines of, "Yes, I have heard of it, but I don't really know what it means."

After Robin had perused the many internet suggestions, scholarly articles, and friendly feedback, she noticed some overlapping keywords: *make, tinker, explore, create, wonder, imagination, independent,* and *collaborate.* She decided to compile these ideas and create her own description of a makerspace:

> A *makerspace* is a place for individuals to explore a variety of items, including but not limited to creative-art materials, electronics, technology, woodworking materials, and recycled and upcycled materials. It is a place to engage the senses and to manipulate materials from their current state into something only the maker can imagine, either independently or with others.

Makerspaces sparked Robin's curiosity. She thought about what a makerspace would look like in an early childhood classroom and how children and teachers would react and respond to it. That fearless spark drove Robin to bring the idea to our early childhood team and enlist the efforts of Teresa, Sarah, Cathy, and several other team members to initiate the maker movement in early childhood programs in the state of Nevada. It began with the introduction of pop-up makerspaces. The movement grew and flourished as a number of early childhood programs added makerspaces to their early childhood programs. This book shares the many lessons we have learned and highlights how you can make space for a makerspace in your early childhood program.

Here is what some early childhood directors, teachers, and families had to say about being part of an early childhood makerspace:

> "Since being introduced to Makerspace, each of our classrooms has created a Makerspace area of their own. I have seen firsthand how Makerspace promotes cooperative play, vocabulary development, and creative expression. I am excited to have the opportunity to offer Makerspace in each of our classrooms, as it fosters a whole-child learning approach." —Amy Benson, center director

> "My son loves using his hands and creating, so it is great that he is able to do this in his classroom. Seeing him talk to his friends about what he was creating while they shared about their own projects was amazing. He gets so excited when sharing with me about what he and his friends create in the classroom. As a parent, I like seeing my child being able to use his own strength as part of his learning. It was great to see the excitement from the children as they interacted." —Erin Skaggs, preschool parent

> "For me, the makerspace learning approach is an eye-opening, mind-blowing way to look at how children learn. It takes children's learning experience to a new level. At first, most children did not know what to do and kept asking for instructions. It was a new kind of freedom, and they had to use their brains to imagine and use their critical-thinking skills. Children seemed more engaged and had longer playtime, which resulted in some awesome conversations and storytelling." —Sophia Oh, preschool teacher

> "The children in my classroom loved every minute of makerspace. They were always excited and would just jump in and start doing things. They were very engaged with the makerspace materials and did things I never thought of doing. Makerspace gave the children the opportunity to be creative, and observing that was my favorite part." —Charlee Wright, preschool teacher

Keep reading to learn more about how you can enhance your early childhood program with makerspace experiences.

⚙⚙ ACKNOWLEDGEMENTS ⚙⚙

We would like to thank all of the people who supported us in the creation of this book. We express gratitude to the early childhood administrators, directors, teachers, families, and children who embraced the concept of makerspaces in early childhood. We are especially grateful to each of our families for their love and support. We want to thank those who provided feedback on our book during its development. We appreciate Danielle Ward for designing the graphic, "Phases of a Maker." A big thanks to the editorial team at Gryphon House, especially Stephanie Roselli. We are especially grateful for our amazing early childhood team who supported our many makerspace experiences.

1

WHY MAKERSPACE? THE BIG IDEA

Preschoolers enter the Explorer room with anticipation and curiosity; they have been told that today they will be involved in a makerspace. As the children move over to the rug for instructions, they see many interesting materials and tools set out on the tables and floor. One table is set up with blueprints, screwdrivers, magnifying glasses, keyboards, and an old desktop computer. Another table is full of natural materials such as pinecones, twigs, acorns, leaves, and shells. Additional tables are filled with creative art supplies and loose parts, including beads and feathers. On the floor is a large toolbox containing real tools, pieces of wood, protective eyewear, measuring tapes, and more.

The materials have been carefully selected and set out for the children. The teacher, Amy, is nervous. She is not sure how the preschoolers will react to the makerspace. A couple of the children in her class often exhibit challenging behaviors if they are not involved in interesting activities. Will the makerspace be too open ended for these children? Will the children engage with the materials without a lot of instructions and guidance? Amy decides to trust the process and see what happens. She is grateful that teachers Trish and Becca are there to help.

As the children walk into the room, Mario exclaims, "Wow!" Stephanie is pointing excitedly at the woodworking tools. Anthony stops and stares at the electronics. Amy smiles and allows the children to take their time to look at all the new things and then settles the children down at the rug. She tells them that today they will have the opportunity to be makers. She reads *The Most Magnificent Thing* by Ashley Spires. After reading the book, Amy tells the children that they can go to any of the tables and use the materials to make their own most magnificent thing. The only rules are to be safe and have fun. Teachers Trish and Becca will be available to help them use the tools safely.

The children cautiously move to the tables. They appear to be waiting for more instructions or directions. When none come, they eagerly jump into making and creating. For almost two hours, the children are engaged in making. They actively create, explore, and try out their ideas. The teachers are close by, providing support and encouragement but not interfering with the process of making. The teachers occasionally ask open-ended questions to learn more about what the children are thinking and doing. Throughout the makerspace experience, the teachers celebrate the many magnificent things the children are creating. Amy is pleasantly surprised at how involved the children are in the makerspace.

This scenario provides a glimpse into a makerspace. As you read this book, you will discover how you can make space for a makerspace in your early childhood classroom. In this chapter we discuss the "big idea" of makerspaces. Next, we look at drafting the plan to create a makerspace for preschool children. After considering the components of your plan, in the third chapter we guide you through the steps of taking inventory of what you have and what you need to supply your makerspace. Chapter 4 presents four different approaches to makerspaces in early childhood programs: tinker trays, interest centers, designated rooms, and pop-ups. We discuss these approaches in detail throughout the book. Next, we elaborate on how makerspaces promote skill development within the developmental domains of young children. Chapter 6 identifies the different "caps" worn by a preschool teacher while facilitating a makerspace experience. In the final chapter we explore the phases that children go through as they are involved in a makerspace experience. The authors offer examples from their work with a variety of early childhood programs over the past couple of years. You will learn about the experiences of Learn and Grow Child Care*, a private, suburban center with about fifty children; Handprints in the Highlands, a private religious preschool with about 125 children in a large metropolitan area; and Sunny Days Preschool, a state-funded child-care program with about sixty children in a rural community.

*The center names are pseudonyms.

⚙️⚙️ BECOMING A MAKER ⚙️⚙️

Making things is not new. Humans have a history of making and creating. Think about the pyramids of Egypt and the Taj Mahal in India. Many of you have probably engaged in one or more do-it-yourself projects. Ask yourself the following questions:

- Do you enjoy making things or tinkering with a new item until you figure out how it works?
- Have you ever been told you are creative?

If you answered yes to either question, you are probably a maker! Makers are individuals who like to make, create, invent, and innovate. Makers build furniture, gardens, pet beds, art displays, and countless other specialty items. Makers have a mindset—a way of viewing the world—as a place to create, to take things apart and put them back together. They know how to persevere and try, try, try again. A maker mindset requires critical thinking, problem solving, and curiosity. As you can see, a maker mindset is imaginative, playful, and curious.

⚙️⚙️ CREATING A MAKERSPACE ⚙️⚙️

The space or surface where we make things is often called a *makerspace*. According to Makerspaces.com, "Makerspace is a collaborative workspace inside a school, library, or separate public/private facility for making, learning, exploring, and sharing that uses high-tech to no-tech tools." Within these locations, specific areas are set up with materials and tools where makers can tinker and share their skills with others. Some makerspaces have specific times set up for collaboration with other makers. Makerspaces in schools encourage students to put learning into practice and to test their ideas. Some community makerspaces are run completely by volunteers, who host events and classes for like-minded people in topic areas such as robotics, woodworking, and metalworking. Some community makerspaces even include specialty items, such as laser cutters and 3D printers, to use for making.

There are many different kinds of makerspaces that can offer a diversity of experiences from coding to sewing, from woodworking to building robots, from inventing to taking apart and exploring materials. In early childhood classrooms, makerspaces will look different, depending on the needs and interests of the children in the classroom.

Makerspaces should reflect the unique interests of the participants within the space. The best types of materials for a makerspace are those that reflect your community and the cultural backgrounds of families within your program. Makerspaces include both permanent tools and consumable materials. Most materials are open ended, and many are relatively inexpensive.

Remember, a makerspace is not a kit. The spirit of a makerspace is to foster creativity and provide opportunities for children to make their own unique and original creations. Barbara Carey, coauthor of *Thinkers and Tinkers: The Maker Movement*, once said, "What do you do with a makerspace? The simple answer is you make things. Things that you are curious about. Things that spring from your imagination . . . that inspire you and things that you admire. The informal, playful atmosphere allows learning to unfold rather than conform to a rigid agenda. Making, rather than consuming, is the focus. It is wonder-driven." A makerspace is a combination of exploratory and constructive play. It involves manipulating materials to see what will happen.

History of Makerspaces

The maker movement is linked to the do-it-yourself culture. The maker movement became more formalized in 2005 with the launch of Dale Dougherty's *Make* magazine. In 2006, Dougherty and his team held the first Maker Faire in San Mateo, California, where more than twenty thousand makers came together to share what they had made. At the Maker Faire, individuals had opportunities to display their creations, converse about their ideas, and celebrate together. In 2016, more than 1.4 million people attended one of the many Maker Faire events held around the world. Whereas in the past makers were more isolated, makers of today are often part of a community of makers. Events such as the Maker Faire have brought people together to collaborate in the making process. Dougherty and others like him continue to build communities of makers with the purpose of elevating creativity, igniting curiosity, and promoting innovation.

The maker movement was also born out of the idea that, although we are not able to predict what future jobs will be needed in our ever-changing world, we can prepare our children for an economy that will value creativity, problem solving, and innovation.

WHY MAKERSPACES IN EARLY CHILDHOOD?

A makerspace in early childhood is an invitation for young children to boldly explore materials and to create something only they can imagine. Children make choices and determine how they want to interact with materials and tools. The experience is multi-dimensional and flexible. According to Judith Van Hoorn, author of *Play at the Center of Curriculum,* "When young children are actively engaged and intrinsically motivated, we observe their zest as well as their focused attention. We see an expression of a child's developing personality, sense of self, intellect, social capacity and physicality." Within a makerspace, children are actively constructing knowledge rather than passively taking in information. They are gaining a stronger sense of self as they initiate the process of turning their ideas into reality.

During the early childhood years, a child's brain is growing more rapidly than at any other time. Children are naturally curious about the world around them. They are interacting with objects and interpreting their experiences as they learn to understand the world. Children's interests, questions, and intentions drive their exploration, their experimentation, and the way they build new knowledge and understanding.

Many teachers who consider adding a makerspace to their classroom face the challenge of how to explain the value that this learning experience provides for children. Coteachers, families, or administrators may ask, "What is the benefit of providing a makerspace for children?"

When observing young children in makerspaces, the benefits for each child who enters and explores become evident.

- Using different materials and tools
- Designing
- Engaging in problem solving
- Learning by doing
- Being persistent
- Thinking critically
- Gaining self-efficacy
- Collaborating with peers
- Creating
- Wondering
- Communicating
- Exploring
- Inventing and innovating
- Connecting to the real world

Most importantly, children have the opportunity to take ownership of their learning and exploration. Makerspaces involve children in self-directed learning. They use trial and error to test their hypotheses, or good guesses. They solve problems. They gain skills in flexible thinking, adaptability, initiative, and collaboration. Children begin to see themselves as creators and inventors. They build confidence in their capacity to actively participate in hands-on learning.

Another strength of the makerspace experience is that children are learning life skills in all of their developmental domains. Their cognitive, physical, and social-emotional development are all enhanced as they participate in these experiences. They are developing social-emotional skills as they regulate their emotions, make responsible decisions, express their ideas, and work both independently and collaboratively with peers. Makerspace experiences can enhance children's physical skills, including gross motor skills that are strengthened as they coordinate their movements to lift and carry materials. Children are increasing their fine-motor skills, eye-hand coordination, and prewriting abilities

Makerspaces and STEM

You may be familiar with the word *tinkering*, which can be defined as "a playful and experimental way to engage with materials and tools." Tinkering involves trying out new possibilities and exploring ideas. It involves learning how things are made and attempting to improve something by making changes to it. When children are tinkering, they are full of focus and purpose—they are seeking solutions. Children learn from their failures and gain the ability to persist through challenges.

While makerspaces can serve as an introduction to science, technology, engineering, and math (STEM), some makerspace experiences include elements of STEM and some do not. Makerspaces encompass much more than STEM and focus on learning through doing within all subject areas. Learners create their own knowledge as they interact with tangible objects and tools. Children may or may not be exploring and experimenting with the fundamentals of STEM, but they are always involved in the creative process of making. Learners ask questions and discuss ideas from a variety of instructional areas as they develop their critical-thinking and social-emotional skills through the creative inquiry process. They have opportunities to work both individually and collaboratively as they engage in the learning process. There is no need to create a specified product. It is a time of discovery and exploration.

as they manipulate materials and tools. Cognitively, children use their mathematical skills to make calculations to design and construct, and use complex thought processes to solve problems. Children can also become very focused in makerspace experiences, which increases their ability to sustain their attention.

When children engage in makerspace environments, they are involved in personalized learning experiences based on their individual interests. Self-directed learning inspires children to become actively involved. They have opportunities to learn from others, as they watch their peers create and make. Curiosity is sparked as they explore a variety of materials and tools. Children are highly interested in makerspace experiences and, therefore, persist longer and are able to take failure in stride. They also gain confidence in their abilities to innovate and invent.

The variety of choices within a makerspace allows children to find something they are comfortable exploring and to create something only they can imagine! It allows children to find materials and tools they have never seen before and tinker with them to gain new understanding of how the world works. A makerspace permits children to observe others and learn by imitating what they see.

Being curious and wonder-driven is important to children's development in all curriculum areas. Children are constructing, inventing, tinkering, manipulating, and dreaming of possibilities. Makerspaces nurture the foundational mindset of a maker and encourage children to create what they imagine without limitations. Makerspaces are designed to be safe places for children to ask questions and explain their ideas to others, to use tools, and to invent new things. Let's look at some of the different types of makerspaces.

TYPES OF MAKERSPACES

TINKER TRAYS

Within an early childhood classroom, a space for making can be as simple as a tray on a table, often called *tinker trays*, where children can access a variety of open-ended materials. Tinker trays could include an assortment of loose parts or screwdrivers with old electronics to invite children to take things apart and put them back together. Loose parts are open-ended materials, such as upcycled tubes and packing containers. To allow for the greatest exploration, provide a plentiful variety of open-ended materials. These

> "Every time we teach a child something, we keep him from inventing it himself. On the other hand, that which we allow him to discover for himself will remain with him visible . . . for the rest of his life."
>
> —Jean Piaget, developmental psychologist

are trays with smaller, carefully chosen makerspace materials that reflect and enhance children's interests. Tinker trays can be set out for a period of time and then easily cleaned up.

POP-UP MAKERSPACE

Another type of mobile makerspace is a pop-up makerspace, which is a great way to introduce the concept of a makerspace to young children. The program or an outside group typically brings this type of makerspace into an early childhood classroom. While the children are in another area of the building, the makerspace is set up, so when the children return to the classroom they have a new area to explore. During the pop-up makerspace experience, adults with previous makerspace experience model how to use the space, and the classroom teachers are active observers and participants. After the designated timeframe, usually 1 to 2 hours, the pop-up makerspace is packed up. Classroom teachers who experience a pop-up makerspace gain a better idea of what a makerspace experience looks and feels like, and they can determine how they want to implement this approach in their classroom in the future. A pop-up is a great way to alleviate or eliminate many of the concerns teachers have about setting up a makerspace experience, because the teachers can see how the children in their class will react.

PERMANENT MAKERSPACE

Some makerspaces take up large rooms; whereas, others are found on one table in a classroom. Some early childhood educators may choose to set up a makerspace in a designated room, such as an extra classroom or a multipurpose room. This provides the opportunity for different groups of children to rotate in and out of the designated area and allows more space to keep large materials set up.

MAKERSPACE CENTER

Other programs include a makerspace in their classroom interest centers. Makerspace centers are set up like other centers, such as the block center or dramatic play area. The makerspace materials are organized on open shelves, and the children are welcome to use them freely during designated times. Like other centers, materials are rotated and changed to maintain children's interest.

⚙⚙ TYPES OF MAKING ⚙⚙

Makerspaces can provide opportunities for different types of making, including tinkering, storymaking, and design challenges. Tinkering happens in all makerspaces. During storymaking, children create stories and props using the available materials to bring their stories to life and then share their stories with each other. Stories can be long or short and should be based on the children's interests. For example, a teacher might hear children talking about an event, an item, or a situation and invite the children to create a story about it. The teacher would then document what the children say or describe and scaffold the children's thought processes by asking intentional, open-ended questions. The teacher might also guide the children to create a timeline of events related to their story. The experience of storymaking can expand children's thinking and vocabulary as they develop and share their story ideas.

A second type of making is solving design challenges. The teacher presents a challenge or problem that the children can solve using the materials in the makerspace. The children are challenged to use their problem-solving skills, imaginations, and creativity to design a solution. For example, the teacher could read a book that poses a problem, such as "How will the animals cross the river?" and then invite the children to work in small groups to create a solution to that problem. Throughout this book, we share more examples of storymaking and design challenges in a makerspace.

The possibilities for children's self-discovery within a makerspace are limitless. You can play a key role in enhancing children's growth and development by providing them with makerspace experiences. Now that we have introduced you to different types of makerspaces and how they can benefit young children's learning and development, we hope you feel inspired to have a maker mindset as you read more about using these spaces in preschool classrooms. In the next chapter we discuss the process of setting up makerspace experiences.

2

DRAFTING
THE PLAN

You are probably wondering where to start with creating a makerspace. A good place to begin is to ask yourself some questions to determine which type of makerspace is right for you and your program.

Consider the following:

- Why are we interested in setting up a makerspace?
- How would a makerspace benefit the children in our program?
- What spaces could we use for a makerspace?
- Will we need additional supervision or adult facilitation during makerspace experiences?
- What materials and tools do we currently have that could be used in a makerspace?
- What materials and tools would we need to acquire for a makerspace?
- How can we ensure the makerspace is accessible to all the children?

- How do we ensure that the makerspace reflects the diversity of the communities we serve?
- How could we involve families?
- How will we evaluate the makerspace experience?

Refer to appendix A on page 118 for the Makerspace Reflection Questionnaire, which will guide you and your team in the process of thinking about and planning for makerspace experiences.

Think about the children in your program. What benefits might the children you teach gain from a makerspace? Lisa Murphy, in her book *On Being Child Centered*, recommends asking yourself three important questions when planning any learning experience.

1. What am I doing?
2. Why am I doing it?
3. Who is it for?

One of the key features of makerspace experiences is that they are set up to be child directed. This means that makerspaces are designed so that the children are taking the lead on what to do and how to do it within a teacher-supported environment. You can even tailor the experience to meet the needs of specific children in your program. For example, you may ask, "How can we set up the makerspace to provide Jordan with time to practice his fine-motor skills?" or "How could we design the makerspace experience to give Samantha opportunities to practice her social skills?" It is important to take time to consider some of the unique benefits each child in your program could experience within a makerspace.

After you have answered the questions about why to have a makerspace and how it will benefit the children in your program, the next step is to consider how you will make it a reality. Take time to consider how you could bring the idea of makerspace to life in your space. It is important to remember that not all makerspaces will look the same and different makerspace blueprints will work for different groups of children. Think about your space and the type of materials you currently have available. Ask yourself the following questions:

- What rooms or locations could you use for a makerspace? Could you rearrange an area in a classroom? Do you have an extra classroom or multipurpose room that might work?

- What are the best days and times for the children to have makerspace experiences (if the makerspace is not a permanent classroom center)? How often will the makerspace be available—every day or only on certain days?
- What materials and tools do you currently have that could be used in a makerspace?
- What additional materials could you add that would be appropriate and culturally responsive to the children in your program?
- What current program policies and procedures do you need to consider when setting up the makerspace?

ASSESSING YOUR SPACE

Let's begin with space. There are several different options for how to set up a makerspace. In this book, we offer four options to help you get started.

- **Tinker Trays**: If space is limited, you can put together tinker trays. These are trays of materials that children can explore and manipulate during designated times or days. A tray could include natural materials, such as pinecones, leaves, and acorns; electronics, such as old computers and cell phones that children can take apart and put back together; or creative-arts materials, such as buttons, tissue paper, and ribbon.
- **Interest Center**: If space is available in the classroom, you can create a makerspace interest center. Similar to a block or a dramatic play interest center, which are set up with a specific focus, the makerspace interest center would offer tools and open-ended materials for making. Children would have opportunities to access this center during free-choice time.
- **Designated Room**: If you have an empty classroom or multipurpose room, you can create a more extensive makerspace. You can set up the room with different types of materials and tools, including woodworking and design, electronics, upcycled materials, natural materials, and creative art materials. Children could go to the room during designated times to tinker and create.
- **Pop-up**: If you want to try out a makerspace experience to see how children will react to it, you could do a pop-up makerspace in your classroom for a few hours. Pop-up makerspaces are set up for a designated period and then taken down. This would give you an opportunity to observe the children in a makerspace and learn more about this type of experience.

Some programs start out with tinker trays or a pop-up makerspace and then progress to interest centers and designated rooms. Other programs begin with an interest area or designated space. You can decide which option best suits your program.

As you think about these options and evaluate your space, think creatively. How could you incorporate a makerspace into your classroom or program? Sometimes classrooms have usable space that they do not even realize is available until after they really examine their space. The following is an example of how Robin, one of the authors of this book, helped Handprints in the Highlands look more closely at their classroom space. This classroom included children ages three to five years old.

> As Robin entered the classroom, she stood at the door and began to evaluate the space. She observed the preschoolers and teachers moving throughout the room and looked at the traffic flow and interest centers that were occupied. She noticed a fairly large corner in the back of the classroom that housed a drying rack and sleeping mats. Robin asked the teacher, Callie, about the space and was told that the space was used to store items the children were no longer interested in using. Robin made a sketch of the classroom and started thinking about how that extra space could be turned into a makerspace interest center.
>
> Later that afternoon, Robin met with the classroom teachers and asked them to think about their space and how they might use it more efficiently. They spoke about the flow, the centers, and the spaces that were not being utilized. During the conversation, Robin and the teachers started moving some of the furniture. They placed unused items into storage and repositioned the tables. Once this was done, they had created an ideal space for a classroom makerspace interest center.

Sometimes it may seem like you do not have any space to spare; however, with creativity and some rearranging, you may be able to find the ideal spot for a makerspace.

As mentioned earlier, throughout this book we will follow three programs as they implement different types of makerspaces. Learn and Grow Child Care had limited space and decided to use tinker trays on what they called Tinker Tuesday. Each Tuesday, the teachers pulled out their makerspace carts and set up tinker trays around the room. Children had opportunities to interact with a variety of materials that were set out on trays and found in the carts. At Handprints in the Highlands, Callie found space in her classroom to create a makerspace interest center. At Sunny Days Preschool, they had an extra classroom that they transformed into a designated makerspace. Because there is no "one size fits all" makerspace model, you have the freedom to decide what kind of makerspace will work best for your program and the children in your classroom. You can also start small and grow your makerspace over time.

 # CONSIDERING YOUR PROGRAM'S PHILOSOPHY, POLICIES, AND PROCEDURES

Makerspace experiences can be implemented in any program and can complement any philosophy or curriculum. One of the first things to consider is your "why" behind implementing a makerspace. Understanding your why will help you align a makerspace with your program's philosophy.

For example, Learn and Grow Child Care has a child-focused, play-based philosophy that emphasizes the importance of purposeful play to children's development. Some of the components of a play-based philosophy include children learning through their efforts, personal decision making, and choices. This educational approach easily aligns with implementing a makerspace. While children participate in the makerspace, teachers can observe how the children work and play. These observations are then used to design lesson plans based on the children's interests and emerging skills.

Handprints in the Highlands implements a theme-based curriculum that features specific topics of focus, such as pets or community helpers. With this type of curriculum, teachers can connect the materials in the makerspace with their themes. They add additional materials to the makerspace to complement their themes.

Sunny Days Preschool has a cognitive-based philosophy, which means that the classroom environment is set up so that children are learning through active engagement with materials. Children are encouraged to be curious and become creative thinkers—a philosophy that matches the key components of a makerspace. Teachers can document the cognitive development of the children during makerspace experiences.

Although the program philosophies of all three centers align with implementing makerspace experiences, not all recommended makerspace materials and tools fit all of the programs' policies and procedures. For example, at Handprints in the Highlands, they had policies against using scissors and tape dispensers without close teacher assistance.

This required the teachers to modify their makerspace to match these guidelines. Similarly, Learn and Grow Child Care had certain procedures that restricted the use of real tools in the classroom, so the teachers decided to focus on creating different types of tinker trays for their makerspace experiences. It is important to review your program's policies and procedures, as well as health and licensing guidelines, when you are planning your makerspace. Be open to adapting your makerspace to fit the specific guidelines of your program.

CREATING A MAKERSPACE FOR ALL CHILDREN

When planning the makerspace, consider children's families—their interests, previous experiences, and particular needs—and the children's learning preferences. It is important to create an inclusive environment by considering simple accommodations and modifications that will ensure that all children can fully participate.

What does an inclusive makerspace for all children look like? Consider these four factors when answering this question:

- Family engagement, influence, and culture
- Children's interests and previous experiences
- Children's learning preferences
- Accommodations for exceptional children

FAMILY ENGAGEMENT, INFLUENCE, AND CULTURE

We first look to families for information about their child. According to the National Association for the Education of Young Children (NAEYC), "Programs and families benefit from shared resources and information. Programs can invite families to share their unique knowledge and skills and encourage active participation in the life of the school. Teachers can seek information about children's lives, families, and communities and integrate this information into their practices." Consider inviting families to share items such as pictures and mementos from their homes. Be culturally responsive by giving families opportunities to share stories about their cultures.

According to the IRIS Center, a national center dedicated to improving education outcomes for all children, "Cultural responsiveness is the ability to learn from and relate respectfully with people of your own culture as well as those from other cultures." Children attending your program are likely to have varied family structures, socioeconomic statuses, and cultural and ethnic backgrounds, as well as live in diverse communities. Every group of children is unique in how they develop and learn. Effective practices for working with children from diverse backgrounds include validating children's cultural identity and promoting equity and mutual respect for all children. Culturally responsive programs bridge the gap between home and school by investing time and energy in building connections with families.

Culturally responsive practices align with the NAEYC guidelines for developmentally appropriate practices. Within makerspace experiences, children have opportunities to develop independence, self-concept, self-esteem, and verbal communication. Tailor the makerspace experiences to match the unique needs of the children and families that your program serves.

A family questionnaire can provide rich information to guide planning for experiences in the makerspace. You may consider the following questions to include in a family questionnaire:

- What activities in the home is your child most interested or involved in? For example, does your child enjoy building with Legos or blocks, drawing, playing games, or pretend play?
- How does your child typically interact with other children? Does your child play alone, alongside (but not necessarily with) other children, or cooperatively?
- What languages are spoken in your home?
- What types of jobs do family members have?
- How does your family celebrate important events, such as birthdays, holidays, and cultural celebrations?
- Do you have some things that reflect your culture and background that you are willing to show or share with us in the classroom? For example, would you be willing to share talents, hobbies, pictures, tools, or stories?

See appendix B on page 121 for a sample family questionnaire. You can adapt the questionnaire to meet the needs of the families in your program. We have found that most families are supportive of makerspace experiences and see value in their child's involvement. It is helpful to provide the families with information that includes a brief description of makerspace experiences and the benefits children will gain. It is also beneficial for families to see their child's progress during makerspace experiences. You can provide families with photos and descriptions about what children are working on and what children are saying as they create their unique items.

Families can also be involved in makerspace experiences by donating materials and tools. Sometimes the makerspace experience even ripples into children's homes. One teacher shared that she had a family that frequently brought in items such as paper-towel tubes to be used in the classroom makerspace. After some time, the teacher noticed that the family had stopped bringing the items in. When she followed up with the family, the child's mother sent her a picture of the child doing makerspace activities at home with the paper-towel tubes and other materials. The child liked the makerspace experience so much that he wanted to continue it at home.

It is rewarding for a teacher to see the ideas promoted in the classroom being used at home. What a great joy it is for families to have the experience of being involved in a makerspace together. While many families may not embrace the idea of a makerspace in their home, it is important for teachers to share pictures and stories from makerspace experiences at school with families. Hopefully, this will encourage families to appreciate the creativity and innovation of young children.

CHILDREN'S INTERESTS AND PREVIOUS EXPERIENCES

The second factor to consider is children's interests and previous experiences, as illustrated in the following vignette:

> Tommy's older brother takes him fishing in the summertime at the pond near their home. Tommy has learned how to hold a fishing rod, cast the fishing line, and then turn the reel to wind the line. Tommy's preschool friend Quinn has never experienced fishing, and when she sees the parts and pieces of a fishing rod and reel in the makerspace, she is not interested. In contrast, Tommy is thrilled to see the fishing-rod materials and quickly works to assemble the parts.

Tommy asks Quinn if she would like to help him, and he proceeds to describe his experiences of fishing with his brother and how to use the rod and reel.

In this scenario, the teacher gained information from a family questionnaire describing Tommy's fishing experience, and she included fishing materials in the makerspace. Joanne Hendrick, author of *The Whole Child*, states, "The more varied experiences children have in their lives, the wider the range of creative expression. The more personal experiences children have with people and situations outside of their own environment, the more material they can draw on to incorporate into their play." Makerspaces give children opportunities to have new experiences and to expand their creative expression.

Planning a culturally responsive makerspace includes offering plenty of opportunities for creative thinking based on the children's interests and ideas, as illustrated in this vignette:

When four-year-old Sawyer visited his great-grandmother's home on the Navajo reservation, he saw drawings in the rocks. He learned from his great-grandmother that the drawings, or *petroglyphs*, were made by his ancestors long ago. Sawyer quickly became interested in creating his own petroglyphs. He carried his interest into the class makerspace, where he used a variety of materials to create his own drawings.

This example shows that a child's interests and ideas can be influenced by his background. Teachers can learn more about each child by having casual conversations with family members and asking children to share their experiences. Obtaining responses from a family questionnaire can also open a window into the types of things children are interested in exploring.

CHILDREN'S LEARNING PREFERENCES

The third factor for creating an inclusive makerspace encompasses individual learning preferences. Here is an example of how one teacher ensured her makerspace allowed for a child's individual preference.

While engaged in the makerspace interest center at Handprints in the Highlands, Dawnie stood next to a tray of paints and various objects that could be used with the paint, such as bubble wrap, a paper-towel tube, a foam brush, and disposable cups. Miss Earnen knew that Dawnie had a sensitivity to sensory experiences and did not like the way paint felt on her hands. Miss Earnen observed Dawnie for a few minutes and then asked if she would like to paint. Dawnie looked at the paint and then back to Miss Earnen. Understanding the child's unspoken concern, Miss Earnen took some disposable gloves from the cabinet and helped Dawnie put them on. She then encouraged Dawnie to use the various objects in the paint and create something spectacular. Dawnie looked at her teacher with a slight smile and began to smear the bubble wrap with paint.

Teachers need to be aware of children's preferences and create an environment that includes quiet spaces for children who like the quiet and more active spaces for those children who do not mind noise. Your space may have carpeted areas where children can stretch out, soft beanbag chairs to sit in, and a mix of bright and natural lighting for children who prefer one or the other.

Some children prefer to work alone while others like to work with another child. Some children may love to move around while others can sit still for long periods. Some children take their time when they encounter new materials, and others quickly jump into their tasks. It is important for teachers to be responsive to each child's individual needs and preferences and to understand that learning preferences and culture are connected with life experiences.

Five-year-old Maya is being raised by her grandmother, an accomplished weaver. Maya has spent many hours rolling homemade yarn into balls while watching her grandmother weave a rug on a loom. Because of Maya's life experience within her culture, she was excited to see yarn and other familiar materials set out on tinker trays in her classroom.

Remember to be flexible as you create a space that meets the individual needs and preferences of the children in your classroom.

ACCOMMODATIONS FOR EXCEPTIONAL CHILDREN

The fourth factor to consider is how to meet the needs of exceptional children. Think about how your center currently addresses accommodations. Will all children be able to move around the makerspace and acquire items independently—even while using a wheelchair or walker? How will you support children with social anxiety? Will they be expected to work collaboratively, or will you have opportunities within the makerspace to work independently? What about a child who has trouble communicating? Will he be able to access materials if he is unable to tell you what he wants or needs?

> While in the makerspace interest center, four-year-old Devin stood with his hands over his ears watching his classmate hammer a nail into a piece of wood. He then moved to another area where children were taking apart an old remote control using screwdrivers. Devin plugged his ears when he heard the scraping noise of the tools on metal. His teacher noticed Devin moving from one activity to another with his ears covered. She knew from previous observations that unusual or loud noises could be overwhelming for him. She also was aware that Devin enjoyed doodling and drawing pictures. As part of her makerspace, the teacher had included blueprints and pictures of buildings as well as writing and drawing materials. She approached Devin and, while pointing to the materials, she asked, "Devin, what do you think you could create using these?" She explained how a blueprint is used to design a building and then gave him the choice of moving the materials to a quiet space. In the quiet area, Devin's interest was sparked, and he began drawing an outline of a building.

The teacher's understanding of Devin allowed him to participate in the makerspace in a way that accommodated his individual needs. She planned to slowly introduce tools that make noise so that Devin could still have those experiences and become more comfortable with them over time.

Gina Seymour, author of "8 Ways to Build a More Inclusive Makerspace," advises that the placement of materials and arrangement of access and passageways should be viewed through the lens of children whose abilities may require accommodations. Take time to view your space through the eyes of the children who will be participating in the makerspace. Can they reach materials easily? Can children in a walker or wheelchair get around without obstacles as they maneuver through the space? Are there any tools or materials you could include that would make their experience richer and more satisfying? Make the appropriate accommodations for children who need help using or accessing the materials, such as setting up materials at different levels for children who are not yet walking or have limited mobility. Consider any accommodations and modifications that would help all the children who use the space to have a positive and enriching experience.

> Jared, a three-year-old with Down syndrome, was excited to explore the materials on the tinker trays during makerspace. He used his walker to help support him as he stood near the table. Jared lined up the craft sticks, colorful ribbons,

and cardboard circles while laughing and making eye contact with his teacher, Daniel. Jared soon became tired of standing and sat down on the floor near the table. Daniel quickly moved the tinker tray to the floor and sat with Jared so he could continue exploring the materials that he was interested in.

Makerspace experiences are open-ended and can be easily modified to meet the needs of all children. Makerspaces should be child centered and should allow children to make choices and explore at their own pace. As you create your makerspace, remember to consider family influence, culture, previous experience, individual learning preferences, needs, and necessary accommodations for all children.

PUTTING IT ALL TOGETHER

Once you have taken time to consider the different aspects of a makerspace, you can begin to draft your plan. In appendix C on page 123 is a form that you can use to begin planning. You will need to consider where, when, what you have, and what you need to set up a makerspace. We also offer several examples of completed program planning guides in appendix C.

To give you a clearer picture of what it could look like to use the program planning guide, let us eavesdrop on the planning process at Handprints in the Highlands. The director, Mr. Emilio, and preschool teachers Miss Earnen and Miss Callie are meeting to draft their plan. Earlier they had each completed the makerspace reflection questionnaire.

Mr. Emilio: Thank you for meeting with me to develop a plan for our makerspace. I would like us to complete the program planning guide together. First, we need to determine where our makerspace will be located and what steps we need to take to prepare the space.

Miss Earnen: We'd like to set up the makerspace as an interest area in our classroom. Callie and I rearranged a few things in the room, and we now have space to create a makerspace interest area.

Mr. Emilio: That's great to hear. It sounds like you have started the process of setting up the space. What else needs to be done?

Miss Callie: We need to add materials and tools to the space. It would be great to have some carts to store the materials. Are there any funds we could use to purchase these items?

MR. EMILIO: Yes, there are some funds that we can use. In a few minutes, we'll need to look more closely at what we have and what we need. When are you planning to give children opportunities to engage in the makerspace? daily? once a week?

MISS EARNEN: We're planning to create a makerspace as one of our interest areas, so it will be available every day during free-choice time. We're still thinking about how to introduce the space to the children once it is set up.

MISS CALLIE: And we also need to plan activities, questions, and challenges that align with our monthly themes.

MR. EMILIO: Yes, I am glad that you're planning to incorporate your classroom's monthly themes within your makerspace interest area. What materials, tools, and storage do we currently have that you could use in your makerspace?

MISS CALLIE: We have a number of interest boxes with open-ended materials that could be used.

MISS EARNEN: We also have a few tools, such as clipboards and measuring tapes, and I have some scissors and hole punches that children could use with adult supervision. There are two shelves in the area where we can store some of the materials.

MR. EMILIO: It sounds like we have some things to get us started. What else do you think you will need?

MISS EARNEN: It would be really great if we had some carts to store the materials. I would love to add natural materials, such as shells, pinecones, and wood disks to our makerspace.

MISS CALLIE: And it would enhance the experience if we added some upcycled materials, such as plastic bottles, cardboard boxes, and paper-towel tubes. I know our children could be really creative using these materials.

MISS EARNEN: Callie, wouldn't it be great if we added some woodworking materials and tools?

MISS CALLIE: Yes! It would be great.

MR. EMILIO: It sounds like you have lots of great ideas. Do you think the families of the children in your class could donate any of these materials?

MISS EARNEN: I'm sure our families would be able to donate some materials, and they might have some tools or other items that they would be willing to give us. We'll need to ask and see what they have available.

Mr. Emilio: Wonderful. By next week, can you create a list of materials, tools, and storage items that you would like to purchase? (Earnen and Callie nod.) Please include the costs and vendors, and I'll see what we can do to build your makerspace. We probably won't be able to purchase all of the materials on your list, but we can start getting some of them. Can you also indicate the items with the highest priority?

Miss Earnen: We will. Thanks.

As seen in the planning process at Handprints in the Highlands, there are a number of things to consider. When drafting your plan, it is best to work together with your team to develop the action steps to take and designate who will take the lead on each action step. Use the program planning guide to get you started. In the next chapter, we will look more closely at the types of materials you could include in your makerspace.

⚙⚙ ADDRESSING CONCERNS ⚙⚙ FROM OTHER TEACHERS, ADMINISTRATORS, AND FAMILIES

There are many benefits to offering children makerspace experiences, but you may also have some concerns. Anytime you add something new to your program, directors, teachers, and families may be wondering about the cost, safety, or structure of the initiative. Let's take a look at seven common concerns about makerspaces and consider some suggestions on how to address these concerns.

"THE DIRECTOR WILL NOT LET ME SET UP A MAKERSPACE."

If you are worried that your director will object to creating a makerspace in your classroom, think about the positives of providing this creative opportunity for the children, and determine the action steps you can take.

Teachers may believe that the administrators at their child-care center will be opposed to the idea of a makerspace. This belief may be related to the program's philosophy, curriculum, or policies. Throughout this book, we address how a makerspace can be implemented in a variety of programs with different philosophies and curriculums. When you meet with resistance, it may be best to share the why behind your idea.

Describe the reasons you feel the makerspace will benefit the children in the program. Communicate your vision of children's involvement in a makerspace and the skills they will be gaining while they are participating. Although you may be imagining an entire room full of materials with children engaged in a makerspace for as much time as they are interested, others may not fully understand your vision. It may be necessary to start small and begin by providing children with trays of materials that they can explore and tinker with. Take photos, write anecdotes, and document the learning that is happening. Then share your documentation with others to show the value of makerspace experiences for young children.

"THE CHILDREN WILL BREAK OR WASTE EVERYTHING."

Individuals may express concerns about children being more interested in destructive play than constructive play. This is sometimes true when children are exploring new materials for the first time. Setting up a new makerspace is exciting for children, and the first time they explore the materials and tools, they may lack focus and direction. Children need time to explore. It may be helpful to start small and add materials as children gain experience with the makerspace. It is beneficial for teachers to take time to talk about the materials and then observe how the children interact with the materials. To help children be successful in a makerspace, set clear expectations, give the children time to explore, and look for hidden benefits. Here is an example of one teacher's experience.

Charlee, a preschool teacher, said that the first time she put out tape for the children, Marcus, a three-year-old child in her class, spent 40 minutes playing with the tape, unrolling it, sticking it to himself, and then discarding it. Charlee worried that Marcus was just wasting the tape.

After discussing the situation with her coach, she began to see the value of the child's exploration. As Marcus was exploring the properties of the tape, Charlee went over and sat on a small chair next to him. She asked him questions about the tape and then offered to hold the pieces he was discarding. She rolled the tape around her fingers as she observed what Marcus was doing. Marcus noticed Charlee using the tape in a new way and began to imitate her. Charlee began to describe Marcus' actions aloud as she continued to observe him interacting with the tape. Over time, as Marcus had more experiences with the tape, he began to use it in different ways, such as making cardboard structures and paper balls.

> Charlee realized that Marcus's explorations with the tape were not wasteful. His exploration taught him about the properties of tape, developed his fine-motor skills, and helped him problem solve as he learned how to determine the right amount of tape he would need for each task. Charlee's gentle guidance provided Marcus a chance to learn these skills on his own and gain the confidence to master new skills.

Additionally, it is beneficial for teachers to set clear expectations on how to use materials. This includes giving children sufficient guidance on the respectful use of tools. When children are engaged with and interested in items, they rarely break the items or are destructive. It is important to give children sufficient time within a makerspace to explore and experiment with materials and tools.

"SOME OF THE MAKERSPACE MATERIALS LOOK LIKE JUNK, AND THE ROOM WILL GET MESSY."

Teachers may be concerned that a makerspace experience with preschool-aged children will get messy. Makerspace experiences often use recycled materials and encourage the children to cut, tape, and take apart the provided materials. Some teachers may be uncomfortable using items that they consider to be junk; however, teachers should be encouraged to try using the upcycled and open-ended materials and to observe how children use the materials. Making choices, problem solving, and sharing ideas will help strengthen young children's cognitive and communication skills.

Teachers should also remember that using and reusing materials teaches children about conservation and upcycling. Although items such as paper-towel tubes, cardboard boxes, and packing materials take up space and are not always as pleasing to look at as manufactured toys and puzzles are, children benefit from opportunities to explore open-ended materials. One of the benefits of these materials is that they allow children the freedom to choose how to use them. Focus on the benefits of using upcycled and open-ended materials.

Implement a storage solution to reduce the mess. For example, one teacher liked the idea of providing a makerspace in her classroom of four-year-old children, but she did not want the upcycled items to be visible after clean-up time. Her solution was to keep all the cardboard items in a large plastic bin covered with a lid when they were not in use.

"A MAKERSPACE IS CHAOTIC."

Teachers may worry that a makerspace will be chaotic and that they will struggle to maintain control of the environment. Makerspaces are designed for active learning, and that can sometimes seem chaotic. Makerspace experiences are child directed, and children are encouraged to use materials in creative ways. This can result in children doing their own thing and becoming immersed in the activity they choose. Often, teachers fear that this will lead to a classroom that is difficult to manage. However, usually the opposite takes place as children become very involved in exploring and making.

The goal of a makerspace is for children to create anything they can imagine and to develop their skills during self-directed play and exploration. This requires that teachers relinquish some control and follow the children's lead. However, this does not mean that there will be chaos. Instead, children take the lead in directing their learning experiences. Set clear expectations, but allow children the time and space to be creative. Remember, the role of the teacher changes slightly in a makerspace. The teacher's role is to ask intentional questions to gain a greater understanding of the child's thinking and to scaffold learning. (We discuss the teacher's role in more depth in chapter 6.)

Consider starting small and introducing makerspace materials a little bit at a time. Ensure that you have plenty of adult support during the first few times you introduce children to a makerspace. Ask for family volunteers or bring in an extra staff member. As children have more opportunities to explore the makerspace, they will become comfortable with the expectations and the freedom to be innovative. With time, there will be a feeling of calm focus and very little chaos in the makerspace.

"FAMILIES DO NOT UNDERSTAND THE BENEFITS."

Teachers may be concerned that families will not understand why having a makerspace is beneficial. Some families may believe that worksheets and product-focused art are concrete proof of learning and may not see the value of more open-ended learning experiences.

Provide families with information on makerspaces and the benefits they offer to children. Invite them to come join in the makerspace with their children. Model asking the children open-ended questions, and encourage them to do the same. Invite them to observe and to allow the children to make decisions. It is also a great idea to take photos and document the learning happening as children are engaged in makerspace activities.

Often, when families observe a makerspace in action and see the amazing hands-on learning happening, they begin to understand its value. It takes time to grasp the why behind a makerspace with young children. Be patient and continue to share the benefits of maker-spaces. The more you believe in the bene-fits of makerspaces, the more you can inspire others to see the value in this type of indepen-dent learning.

"IT'S DANGEROUS."

Teachers and parents may express concerns about introducing real tools or other items to the makerspace that they view as dangerous, especially if the tools require extra safety considerations. Anytime you are introducing tools and materials to young children, you must take precautions. Think about the specific children in your program, and determine what experiences they are ready to have and what tools they may be able to use safely. Do not underestimate the abilities of young children. Young children can successfully use a variety of tools and materials safely, with adequate adult guidance and supervision.

In one program, they introduced a hand drill to a group of four-year-old children, and a small group were very interested in how the tool worked. The children carefully followed the teacher's advice about how to position their hands on the drill and how to work their large muscles as they turned the handle around and around. A few of the children gladly waited their turn so they could try to make a hole in a piece of wood with the drill. The teacher stayed very close by and offered reminders. She made sure the children used the drill safely. The children soon learned how to manage the hand drill without any extra intervention.

The children were self-motivated to learn about the tool, used caution, and persisted to drill through the wood. When considering the safety of the makerspace materials for your group of young children, consider how much supervision the items will require and how you can ensure the experience is safe and successful for the children.

"WE CANNOT AFFORD TO ADD NEW MATERIALS TO THE CLASSROOM."

When planning to add a new center or activity to the classroom, some may worry that they do not have the budget to make it a reality. One great thing about makerspace is that most programs can begin with relatively low costs by using upcycled materials and donations. Have you heard the all-too-common story about how adults purchase an expensive toy for their child, and the child is more interested in playing with the box than the toy? The reason children love to play with boxes is that they are open ended and offer many possibilities.

You do not have to spend lots of money to put together a makerspace for young children. Gather some everyday materials, and encourage the children to create something magnificent. You may be amazed at how they can be resourceful, problem solve, and use the materials in ways that only they imagine.

There are lots of questions to ask yourself and things to consider when setting up a makerspace in your program or classroom. The planning process will continue as you begin to think about the types of materials that you will put in the space. In the next chapter, we discuss taking inventory of what you have available and determining what supplies and tools to add to your makerspace.

3

TAKING INVENTORY AND ADDING SUPPLIES

Once you have drafted your plan, it is time to take inventory of the materials and tools that you have and decide what you will need to add to your makerspace. In this chapter, we detail information on the types of supplies that can be included in a makerspace. We also offer tips for gathering, obtaining, and storing the materials and tools, as well as provide suggestions about how you can request materials from families and the community. As you ponder which items to include in your makerspace, remember that a makerspace is a great place for children to create, invent, explore, and learn how tools work under the watchful eye of an adult. Think creatively and be open to many different possibilities.

With the flexibility afforded by makerspaces, you can set up your space in a number of different ways to meet the unique characteristics of your program as you offer experiences that promote children's autonomy and allow them to use materials and tools in unexpected ways. For example, when Robin, one of the authors, set out some wooden figures in her makerspace, she thought the children would use and reuse them in future makerspace experiences. However, she discovered that the children incorporated the figures into their own creations, so they were not reusable. It is important to be willing to adjust your mindset to meet the needs of the children. Be open and flexible in the types of materials you include in a makerspace as well as how you allow the children to use them. We share examples of the types of materials and tools you could include in a makerspace throughout this chapter.

FOCUS ON THE CHILDREN

As you set up the makerspace, begin by considering the children in your program. They should inspire the types of materials you select and include. Consider the number of children who will be participating, to ensure that you have enough materials and tools. For example, one teacher set up her dramatic play center as a tinker space or woodworking shop to help the children expand their play. She noticed the children using the materials to create baby carriers, wands, crowns, and fishing poles, which gave the teacher clues to their interests and ideas for materials she could add. Another teacher set up her makerspace near the science center to integrate those two topic areas. She discovered children using the magnifying glasses from the science center to examine the materials in the makerspace interest center. She made a note to add some more materials that the children would find interesting.

Ask yourself the following questions:

- What are the children in my program interested in?
- Where are the children developmentally?
- What specific skills are they currently developing, and how could the maker-space experience promote the development of these skills?
- What types of materials and tools could be added to the makerspace to make the experience even more meaningful?

The following is an example of how children's interests inspired a teacher to add specific materials to the makerspace based on what she observed.

Charlee thought about the children in her classroom as she planned the materials to include in her makerspace. One of the families in her classroom owned a boat, and they often invited several other families to go on boat rides. These outings increased several children's interest in boats. Charlee wondered what types of materials she could add to the makerspace that would relate to boats. She began gathering pictures of different types of boats. As the children learned about houseboats, fishing boats, and speedboats, they began to show an interest in building boats of their own.

During a makerspace experience, one group of children gathered materials to build a boat. Mason picked up some craft sticks, cardboard scraps, and tape. He invited his friend Noah to help him as he secured the sticks to the cardboard. When they had worked on the boat for a few minutes, Noah asked Charlee if they could test their boat in the water table. Charlee told them she thought that was a great idea. As the children and Charlee watched the boat in the water, Mason noticed that the cardboard was slowly absorbing the water, and the boat began to sink. Charlee asked the boys if they had any ideas on what they could do. Mason and Noah went back to the makerspace and redesigned their boat several times.

That afternoon, Charlee reflected on the boat making and decided to add some plastic food containers and thicker duct tape to the makerspace for the next day. As she expected, the boat making continued into the next few days, and the children discovered new ways to build boats and make them float. By the end of the week, the children were building all kinds of elaborate boats that could hold various objects as they floated in the water table.

TYPES OF MATERIALS TO INCLUDE IN A MAKERSPACE

You may be wondering about the specific types of materials that work best within makerspace experiences. Let's consider five types of materials:

- Upcycled
- Electronics and technology
- Creative arts
- Woodworking and design
- Natural

UPCYCLED MATERIALS

Upcycling is reusing or updating materials to create items of higher quality or value. Cardboard, water bottles, caps, cans, cups, clean plastic food containers, aluminum foil, paper bags, yarn, string, and tape are common upcycled materials that children can use in the creative process. Other, less common upcycled items include leftover materials from a construction job or home makeover, such as carpet pieces, bath and kitchen tiles, vent hose, and paint samples; household items that are no longer being used, such as a hamster wheel, salad spinner, or lazy Susan; and odds and ends that seem to accumulate in homes and classrooms over time, such as old CDs, ice-cube trays, or shower rings. Many items that may otherwise be discarded can be upcycled and turned into something new during makerspace. The following vignette illustrates how children at Learn and Grow Child Care explored upcycled materials.

Sarah sits on the carpet with a few children who are exploring materials including foam pool noodles that had been cut into rings. The children place various types and colors of rings onto a paper-towel holder. Sophia places a blue ring, then a pink ring, and then a blue ring on the holder, alternating the colors all the way to the top. She is excited that she has filled the holder and shows Sarah what she has done. Sarah comments, "Look, Sophia. You made a pattern; it goes pink, blue, pink, blue, all the way to the top." Sophia's smile grows even wider, and she beckons to her teacher, saying, "Look! I made a pattern all the way to the top!"

Sophia expanded her cognitive skills as she interacted with the materials. Use your imagination and think about the possibilities of different types of materials. Once you begin collecting, you will find that identifying items for upcycling will become easier, and you will begin to think about all the possibilities of what an item could be before you toss it out.

What upcycled materials could you add to your makerspace?

ELECTRONICS AND TECHNOLOGY

Children really enjoy creating something new and different from common materials. They also love to take things apart and explore what is inside, especially items such as electronics and small machines. Adding electronics to a makerspace affords children the opportunity to see how things work and encourages them to be curious and inquisitive. They can investigate what is inside, explore how one wire attaches to another, and discover how gears make different parts move. The following electronic and technology items would be great additions to a makerspace:

- Old video recorders
- Old desktop computer towers (remove the power supply)
- Keyboards
- Computer mice
- Telephones
- Flashlights
- Cameras
- Tape players

See the materials and tools list on pages 36–37 for additional ideas.

Consider reaching out to a few thrift stores to ask if they have some donated electronics that do not work. Often, thrift stores will not be able to sell these types of items, so they discard them. Many stores will gladly let you take these nonworking electronics rather than throw them in the trash.

During a pop-up makerspace, Cedric approaches the table where some old electronic items are displayed along with screwdrivers of various sizes. Cedric picks up the blue screwdriver and starts touching the wires in the old computer. He uses the screwdriver to remove some tiny screws holding a wire in place. He looks at his teacher, Ms. Sang, and asks, "What does this wire do?" Ms. Sang asks, "Have you ever used a computer before?" Cedric replies, "Yes, my dad has one. I play games on his computer." Ms. Sang then asks, "How do you think this wire could be used to help power the computer to play games?" The interaction continues, with Ms. Sang encouraging Cedric to experiment and discover how the computer might work.

MAKERSPACE MATERIALS AND TOOLS

Creative Arts

- Aluminum foil
- Beads: wooden, plastic
- Bubble wrap
- Buttons
- Cellophane
- Chalk
- Chenille stems
- Coffee filters
- Cotton balls
- Craft feathers
- Craft sticks
- Elastic
- Fabric: burlap, cotton, felt
- Foam: floral, peanuts, squares, shapes
- Gems: glass, plastic
- Glue
- Lace
- Paper: construction, tissue, wrapping, bags
- Plastic: threading needles, mesh
- Pompoms
- Ribbon
- Tape: clear, painter's, decorative, floral, duct
- Writing utensils: pencils, colored pencils, markers, crayons
- Yarn

Electronics and Technology

- Blender (blades removed)
- Calculator
- Camera
- Computer
- CDs
- CD player
- Cell phone
- Computer mouse
- DVDs
- DVD player
- Electric fan
- Electric can opener
- Flashlight
- Mixer
- Schematics
- Switches
- Tape player
- Toaster
- TV remote
- Keyboard
- Wire

Household Items

- Baking cups
- Bath or kitchen tiles
- Boxes: cardboard, cereal, tissue
- Brush curlers
- Buckles
- Carpet remnants
- CDs
- Containers: butter, potato chip, wipes, yogurt
- Dryer vent hose
- Hamster wheel
- Ice-cube trays
- Lazy Susan
- Magazines
- Metal: aluminum foil, chicken wire, scrap, wire, cans, foil pans
- Newspaper
- Paint chips
- Paper-towel holder
- Plastic: bottles, jugs, cups, soap dish, bottle caps
- Pool noodles
- Salad spinner
- Shower rings
- Snaps
- Sponges
- Spools
- Sticky notes
- Straws
- Toothpicks

Natural Items

- Driftwood
- Flowers, petals
- Leaves
- Pinecones
- Seedpods
- Shells
- Sticks
- Stones

Woodworking and Design

- Balls: plastic, tennis, wicker
- Baskets
- Clips: binder, paper
- Blueprints
- Board: corkboard, scrap pegboard, corrugated
- Carabiners
- Clay
- Cork
- Fishing rod and reel
- Funnels
- Golf balls, tees
- Kinetic sand
- Lock and key
- Nails, screws
- Nuts, bolts, washers
- Packing material
- Paper: graphing, plates, maps, sand-paper, sketch paper
- Playdough
- Printed photos
- Rubber bands
- Rulers
- Safety pins
- Small cars
- Springs
- Stretchy putty
- String, twine
- Styrofoam
- Tape: magnetic, masking
- Tubes: cardboard, carpet, PVC, plastic, shipping
- Twist ties
- Velcro
- Wood: balsa, scraps, geo shapes, dowels, disks, chips, paint-stirring sticks

Storage Containers

- Baskets
- Buckets
- Cardboard boxes
- Carts: wheeled, stationary
- Drawers
- Large ziplock bags
- Plastic bins
- Shelves
- Toolbox

Tools

- Allen wrench
- Caliper
- Cardboard cutters
- Clamps
- Clipboards
- Computer tools
- Gloves
- Hammer
- Handsaw
- Hole punch
- Level
- Magnifying glass
- Mallet
- Manual hand drill
- Plastic knives
- Pliers
- Pumpkin-carving tools
- Rolling pin
- Safety goggles
- Scissors
- Screwdrivers: flat-head, Phillips
- Stapler
- Stencils
- T square
- Tape measure
- Trays
- Tweezers
- Wire cutters
- Writing utensils: carpenter pencils, pens, pencils

Safety note:
Assess all items for safe use by children in your program.

You can also incorporate current technology into the makerspace experience. Set up a table with a digital camera, tablet, or cell phone that the children can use to take pictures of both their planning processes and completed creations.

Experiment with different digital apps that allow children to film videos using a green screen or create animation and stop-motion animation. Explore some of the coding programs available that support children's exploration of coding and robotics.

What types of electronics and technology could you add to your makerspace?

CREATIVE ARTS

Most children are familiar with creative-arts materials. These open-ended materials often provide the springboard for children's creations, especially when they are new to a makerspace. You can use a variety of materials, depending on the type of makerspace experience you are offering. You may decide to offer children a typical makerspace experience, involve them in storymaking, or give them a design challenge to solve. Some examples of creative-arts materials in a typical makerspace experience include coffee filters, felt, cardboard tubes, chenille stems, construction paper, and other open-ended materials. (We discuss storymaking and design challenges in depth in chapter 4.) The type of experience you choose can guide you as you select materials for your makerspace.

Remember, the best types of creative materials are items that do not have expected outcomes, such as a piece of string or a chenille stem. Children love to use tape, so be sure to include lots of different types, colors, and varieties. Try to find items that are slightly unusual, such as zip ties or plastic rug mesh. Plus, include a variety of more common materials such as tissue paper, feathers, foam squares, wrapping paper, elastic, burlap, floral foam, contact paper, lace, buttons, beads, and yarn. See materials and tools list on pages 36–37 for more ideas.

Students will often create items in a makerspace based on prior experiences. As illustrated in the following example, Tyler used information from things he had seen to create a parachute.

> Tyler spent a considerable amount of time working with the creative-arts materials during an interest-center makerspace experience. He gathered yarn, straws, new coffee filters, and tape. He tugged, tore, taped, and tied until he had created the item that he had imagined.
>
> Tyler's teacher, Ms. Maggie, asked him to tell her about his creation, and Tyler replied, "It's a parachute to help you float to the ground."
>
> "Wow," replied Maggie. "Where have you seen a parachute before?"
>
> "In movies," replied Tyler, "people use them when they jump out of planes."
>
> Maggie replied, "Yes, you're right. Can you show me how your parachute works?" Tyler reached his arm up in the air and then dropped his parachute to the ground.
>
> "It works!" he exclaimed.
>
> "It does work," Maggie agreed. "Can you tell me what materials you used to create your parachute?"

In this example, Tyler had an idea, gathered materials, and constructed a parachute. Then he tried out his idea and it worked. He was able to use a variety of creative-arts materials to create a workable parachute. What types of creative-arts materials could you add to your makerspace?

WOODWORKING AND DESIGN MATERIALS

Some teachers and programs may be hesitant about including real tools within their makerspaces. We hope you will consider how including tools can benefit the children in your program. Real tools are valuable in a makerspace because they teach children how things work. Children really thrive when they have opportunities to use real tools in a meaningful way.

It is important to ensure that safety measures are in place anytime you use tools. Depending on the tools and materials, the children may need to wear safety glasses or protective goggles. At least one adult must be responsible for monitoring children's use of the tools. Make sure that you are comfortable with using the tools yourself prior to introducing them to the children. Take time to show the children how to use the tools correctly, and carefully explain the safety guidelines.

> Ms. Takisha was hesitant to add a rotary cutter to her makerspace because she was not familiar with the tool. She knew that this tool was useful for cutting pieces of cardboard, so she asked her coach to come to her classroom and demonstrate to the children how to use the cutter. After observing the rotary cutter being used safely and using it herself, Ms. Takisha felt more comfortable including it in her makerspace.

Questions to Consider

As you think about the children in your classroom, reflect on the types of materials and tools that you already have available.

- Which ones are open ended? Open-ended materials promote higher levels of creativity.
- How could individual children and small groups use the materials?
- What materials could you acquire that could be dismantled and explored, such as older electronics?
- What tools do you have available that could be used in a makerspace? Consider including woodworking tools.
- What creative-arts materials do you have that would be familiar to the children and could be a springboard for using with less common materials?
- What natural materials might you and the children find in your neighborhood?
- What types of materials and tools might families, friends, and businesses be willing to donate?
- Could you find acceptable and safe materials and tools at a yard sale or secondhand store?

Think about all the different places that you could find materials and tools. Keep reflecting on these questions as you consider the specific types of items that could be included in your makerspace.

Teachers need to be comfortable using any tools they include in a makerspace. Some of the items we have purchased and used in a makerspace include a small home-improvement tool kit, a manual hand drill, an electric screwdriver, a rotary cutter, and cardboard-cutting scissors. Children have used these tools with 2" x 4" wood pieces that had pre-drilled holes for screws and nails. To enhance the woodworking space, we added measuring tapes, clipboards, as well as paper and pencils for documenting experiences during the tinkering process.

In one program, a local architect donated old blueprints. The teachers in the program printed off pictures of local buildings and structures to go along with the blueprints. In another program, a local construction company donated protective goggles for the children to wear. Other items that could enhance the experience include sandpaper, clamps, pliers, levels, nuts, and bolts. See the materials and tools list on pages 36–37 for additional ideas.

What types of woodworking and design materials could you add to your makerspace?

NATURAL MATERIALS

The types of natural materials that are available to you will vary depending on your setting, location, and the time of year. Some programs may have an abundance of natural materials right in their own backyards. Does your environment include fallen leaves, twigs, rocks, or pinecones? Could you invite the children in your program to help gather some of these items for your makerspace?

In one program, the teachers made a masking-tape bracelet for each child, keeping the sticky part on the outside. The children then went on a nature scavenger hunt and collected natural items they found on the playground. The children attached their finds to their tape bracelets or placed larger items in a box. Afterward, the children removed the items from their bracelets and added them to the makerspace. In another program, the teachers invited the children to bring items that they collected when they traveled, such as shells from a beach and seedpods from a park.

Natural materials could include wooden disks (sometimes called *tree cookies*), wicker balls, clay, sponges, and wooden thread spools. See the materials and tools list on pages 36–37 for more ideas. What types of natural materials could you add to your makerspace?

SELECTING THE RIGHT COMBINATION OF MATERIALS

Sometimes the key to a successful makerspace experience is placing the right combination of materials together.

> While Devon was setting up his makerspace in the designated room, he decided to dedicate one table to natural materials, such as sticks, leaves, beans, wooden beads, and a variety of other wooden materials, which he set out on trays. The makerspace offered plenty of space for the children to explore and create. He was excited and thought the children would really enjoy interacting with the natural materials. To Devon's surprise, the children did not share in his excitement. Only one child visited the table briefly and explored the tray with tree wood chips for a short period of time.
>
> Later that day, Devon reflected on the experience and the natural-materials table. He wondered why only one child had visited the table and explored the materials. Why hadn't the children found the items interesting? He decided that the items by themselves did not offer interesting ways to create with them.
>
> During his next makerspace experience, he added some natural, homemade playdough to the natural-materials space. He hoped that this addition would make the natural materials more inviting and engaging. Interestingly, many more children were drawn to the area. The playdough added a new dimension and became the essential base for creating with the natural materials.
>
> Xander began placing beads, beans, and wood chips into the playdough. Devon asked what he was creating, and Xander replied that it was a nest for sea turtles. Xander went on to explain that all the beads, beans, and wood chips were sea turtles and the sea turtles had to sleep for 50 hours and then they would hatch and crawl to the ocean. Devon asked Xander if he had seen a sea turtle before, and Xander said no. Devon then asked him how he knew so much about sea-turtle incubation, and the child excitedly shared all the things he had seen on a nature show about sea turtles.

The addition of one item, natural playdough, expanded children's interactions with the natural materials. As a teacher, do not be discouraged if children do not engage with some of the materials that you set out. Children tend to migrate to the most familiar materials first. With time and encouragement, they will venture out and explore new items. In Devon's case, it may have had more to do with the combination of materials presented than the specific materials. You may have to engage in a little trial and error to discover the right elements for making.

Teacher Callie discovered that natural colored playdough stimulated the children to make many different types of creations. During an interest-center makerspace experience, Luke began adding some natural items to his playdough and then declared himself a baker. Callie asked him what he was baking, and Luke said, "A bean banana pudding cake with chocolate chips." Callie asked Luke what ingredients he needed for his cake, and he said he needed flour, frosting, and decorations. "Have you ever baked a cake before?" asked Callie. "Yes," said Luke, "me and my mom make cakes and watch shows about cakes on TV." Callie asked, "Would you like to write down your cake recipe in case anyone else in our class wants to make a cake?" Luke said he did, and he drew all the ingredients on a piece of paper. Luke told Callie, "I'm going be a baker when I get bigger!"

As you guide children, use your observation and reflection skills to guide you in creating optimum makerspace experiences. Think about the use of the materials and tools from the child's perspective. Ask the children questions about why they select certain materials and not others. Continue to try different combinations of materials until you find the combination that sparks the interest and imagination of the children in your program.

STORAGE AND DISPLAY

Collecting the materials and items for the makerspace is the fun part. Figuring out where to put everything can sometimes be a challenge! Just as each makerspace is unique, so are the storage solutions.

STORING MATERIALS

Whether you are using tinker trays, setting up an interest center, or have a designated room, you will need to evaluate your space and then think about the best way to store the materials and tools. For the pop-up makerspace experiences that we bring into programs, we selected a rolling utility cart. This option allows us to label the containers and separate the items and materials into different categories. These carts easily roll in and out of classrooms and then can be stored conveniently in a room or closet. The following pictures provide visuals of the utility cart we purchased at a local home-improvement store. The cart includes wheels that make it portable and convenient for setting up and taking down a makerspace in an organized manner.

Learn and Grow Child Care chose to add mobile carts to enhance their tinker trays. They filled the carts with additional materials and tools. The children were allowed to move the carts around the room to the different tables where they were creating. The carts helped to keep the materials neat and accessible while also supporting the children's independence and decision-making skills. At Handprints in the Highlands, they had a large storage closet where makerspace materials were stored and added to their makerspace interest center as needed. Sunny Days Preschool had less need for additional storage containers because they had a designated room and closet where the makerspace materials and tools were set up and stored.

There are many different storage options on the market. Spend some time taking an inventory of the materials and tools that you will be including in your makerspace. Think carefully about what types of storage you will need and how you will use each type of storage. Will small materials need individual containers or bins? What would be the best type of container for large items such as cardboard, woodworking tools, and wood pieces?

Do you want to store the materials by type of material, such as creative arts and natural materials, or by size of materials? Look for good quality and moderately priced options. Consider the following factors when selecting storage containers for your makerspace:

- The number of materials to be stored
- The types of materials: tools, recycled and upcycled materials, creative-arts materials, and so on
- Ease of access to materials
- Simple clean-up capability
- Durability and stability: structure, wheels, compartments
- Organization and sorting of materials
- Storage features, such as pullout drawers or shelves
- Space in the classroom for the storage containers or carts

With careful consideration of different types of storage options, you will be able to find the right type of storage solutions for your makerspace.

DISPLAYING CHILDREN'S WORK

You will also need storage and display space for all of the marvelous creations the children design and build. Often makerspace experiences result in some large three-dimensional creations. Children take pride in the things they make and will be reassured knowing there is a place to keep their items safely displayed. Some teachers have designated space on a shelf or table to display the children's creations. Other teachers store creations in cardboard boxes, which can be stored flat until they are needed. Take time to determine the best place for storing and displaying the creations.

As seen in the following photos, one program set up an area for projects that the children were still working on. They also set aside a table where the children could display their finished creations.

> Miss Earnen, a teacher at Handprints in the Highlands, realized the importance of having a display area in the classroom after she found out that one of the families did not want to take home a large creation their child had made. She overheard the parent complaining about the item and saying that it was going into the garbage can as soon as they got home. Miss Earnen wanted to respect the parent's point of view and realized that families may not want to take home everything that their child creates. After that experience, she created

a display area in the classroom where children could place their materials after makerspace experiences. Adding an in-classroom display area was a thoughtful way to show respect for each child's work while also giving the families the option to leave some items in the classroom.

ACCESSING RESOURCES FROM FAMILIES AND THE COMMUNITY

Families are a great resource for enhancing your makerspace. Your community can also be an excellent resource for makerspace materials and tools.

FAMILY INVOLVEMENT

Family involvement is an important aspect of makerspace experiences. Not only can families help out with makerspace experiences, but they can also provide donations. Are any of the members of the families in your program interested in electronics or wood-working? Would they be willing to share their talents with the children in your program? To learn more about the trades and interests of the families in your classroom, you can invite families to complete a family questionnaire (see appendix B on page 121). Additionally, you can use the family questionnaire to request donations for your makerspace.

For your makerspace to be successful, you will need to continually restock materials and tools. Remember the saying "One man's trash is another man's treasure"? Families often have materials and tools that they would be willing to donate, if asked. Another great aspect of family donations is the opportunity to add diversity to the materials you are collecting. Encourage families to donate items that reflect their heritage and home culture. This can help children make connections between home and school. You can also ask families to share stories about the materials and how they are used within their home and culture.

Do not hesitate to ask families if they are willing to donate. Some families may not understand the purpose of their donations, so it is important to give them examples of how items can be used. Include photos and provide families with some guidance on the types of materials and tools that would enhance your makerspace. Appendix D includes sample donation request letters that you can personalize and use for your program.

Before the donations arrive, set aside a designated area or container where families can drop off items. It is usually best to have the collection container outside your classroom so that you can assess the safety of each material before you add it to your makerspace.

COMMUNITY RESOURCES

Local businesses can be a great source of interesting materials. Never underestimate the power of asking. Cathy, one of the authors, had the following experience with one of our local hardware stores.

> Cathy had gone to a local hardware store to purchase some tools for our pop-up makerspace. Standing in the tool aisle, feeling overwhelmed by all the options, she started selecting some multitool kits that included a hammer, screwdrivers, and a tape measure. While pondering how many kits to purchase, the department manager stopped by and asked if she needed any assistance. Cathy explained that she was purchasing tools for young children to use in a makerspace in an early childhood classroom. The store manager asked how the children would be using the tools, and Cathy shared that the children would learn how to use the tools safely and would make real-life connections. The manager was very excited to hear about makerspaces and gave some suggestions of what types of tools to purchase. He also said that he would give her 50 percent off the price of the tools. He invited Cathy to find him the next time she needed to purchase items for the makerspace and said he would provide her with a discount.

Connecting with community partners is a great way to add materials and tools to your makerspace. See appendix D for a sample letter you can personalize and use to request donations from local businesses.

DONATIONS AND SAFETY

Safety should always be a priority when reusing donated materials. Examine each item to ensure it meets your state health and licensing requirements, as well as your program guidelines. Look for age recommendations, such as "Not recommended for children under three." Inspect safety labels on fabric products and art materials. Only use items identified as being safe for young children. Remember, what may be safe for an adult may not be safe for a child.

For tool donations, always keep in mind the current abilities of children in your program to handle tools; however, do not underestimate what children can do under the close supervision of a watchful adult.

ITEMS TO AVOID

Items such as toilet-paper tubes and egg cartons can be breeding grounds for bacteria and should not be used. Avoid using food items, both out of safety concerns and out of respect for diverse audiences. Some children may have allergies, and children from some cultures may not be allowed to handle certain foods. Additionally, avoid using items such as empty medicine bottles and containers that held cleaning solutions or any type of toxic substance. Take time to periodically check the items in your makerspace for potential hazards. Have any items become broken or damaged? Be mindful and watchful to ensure the optimal safety for the children as they engage in a makerspace.

In this chapter, we provided ideas on how to take inventory to determine the types of materials, tools, and storage containers to include in your makerspace. We encourage you to reach out to families and the community to enhance your makerspace. The next chapter shares ideas on how to introduce the makerspace to the children in your program.

4

CREATING THE BLUEPRINT

Blueprints provide building contractors with information that they will need to build a project. Just as contractors need blueprints, early childhood educators need to have a guide or plan for setting up makerspace experiences in preschool classrooms. In your plan, it is important to include guidance on how to set the stage for the makerspace experience by establishing expectations for safety and interactions. It is also important to include ideas on how to introduce makerspace experiences to young children to ensure positive outcomes. In this chapter, we share ideas on how to set up the makerspace, establish expectations, and maintain children's excitement for makerspace experiences.

 # SETTING UP THE MAKERSPACE

As mentioned in the previous chapter, how you set out the materials can make a difference in how the children interact with them. Take time to think about how each of the items you select could be used in making. When we set up a makerspace, we initially group similar types of materials together. Once the makerspace experience begins, children can move the materials to any area in the classroom. Your setup will depend on the type of makerspace experience you have selected.

SETTING UP TINKER TRAYS

We recommend setting out one tinker tray for each child in the classroom. If other makerspace options, such as an electronics interest center, are available, you could set out fewer trays. Place a variety of materials on each tray, and put the trays on a table.

We also include accessible rolling carts with additional materials that the children can use in their making.

SETTING UP A MAKERSPACE INTEREST CENTER

Interest centers are a purposeful way of dividing a classroom into different subject or learning areas; think of your block interest center, reading or library interest center, or dramatic play interest center. In their article "Setting Up Your Preschool Learning Centers" (2021), Kaplan Early Learning Company suggests, "Young children learn best by experimenting with their environment through hands-on activities and play, which is why learning centers are such a vital part of the preschool classroom."

The interest-center space is a clearly defined area arranged for a small number of children to engage with specific types of materials at one time. Children can freely select items to explore while in the interest center. You can define a makerspace interest center by using rolling shelves and mobile carts. Consider having tables without chairs in this interest center so children can move about fluidly. Unrestricted space allows children the ability to move the mobile carts as needed and select materials easily. You may also want to have an area rug for building and making. This arrangement can also support the needs and mobility of all children in your program.

Including a makerspace interest center adds to the options children can explore during free-choice time. This takes some initial planning. You will need to evaluate the room's physical spaces to assess its strengths and limitations, and you will need to choose materials carefully. Ideally, the space should be as flexible as possible: similar to those in the other interest centers in the classroom, the makerspace interest-center materials should be changed periodically based on the children's interests. For example, if the children hear a book about robots, you could add aluminum foil, gears, and electronic parts to the makerspace interest center. Later, if the children are interested in architecture or building, you could add pieces of wood, nails, screws, blueprints, and tools. Additionally, if the children are interested in role play, you could add fabric, ribbon, and hook-and-loop adhesive to the center for children to create costumes. The possibility of materials to add is endless.

Display the materials in a way that invites exploration, such as on trays, directly on a table, or even on the floor. Consider stocking a cart or shelves in the interest area with a variety of additional materials and tools. Rotating items regularly facilitates problem solving and invites children to try something new. You might store makerspace materials in containers based on the type of material, such as consumables, natural materials, electronics, or tools. Look for interesting containers with multiple sections.

> The teachers in the three-year-old class at Handprints in the Highlands offer a variety of interest centers, including a makerspace. The interest centers are developed around a thematic curriculum, and the classroom schedule dictates the amount of time available for children's exploration. Miss Callie especially enjoys science, and she hopes to spark the children's interest in science, math, and technology with the makerspace.
>
> The teachers use a rolling shelf that can be moved around the area for children's ease and accessibility. The children can explore trays of materials set on tables, as the teachers observe them and inspire thinking by asking higher-level questions. The three-year-old children engage with the maker materials for long periods and without any challenging behaviors.

SETTING UP DESIGNATED ROOMS

To set up a designated room, you can place materials and tools on both shelves and tables. If you have four tables available, you could set out a variety of creative-art materials with corresponding tools such as scissors, hole punches, and pencils on one table. Another table could contain trays and bins with upcycled items, such as cardboard tubes and plastic containers. A third table could hold natural materials and playdough, and electronic and technology items could be displayed on the fourth table. Corresponding tools should be available in each area. For example, in the electronics and technology area, include tools such as small screwdrivers, tweezers, and magnifying glasses. We recommend setting up the woodworking and design materials on a rug so that the children have space to build. It is also easier for children to use tools and design items closer to the floor. Remember to inspect the space after each makerspace experience to determine which items need to be replaced or restocked.

SETTING UP POP-UP MAKERSPACES

Pop-up makerspaces are usually set up for a special event by a program or outside group. They are designed to allow children to enjoy the makerspace experience for a few hours; then, the pop-up makerspace is packed up and removed from the space. Pop-up makerspaces are set up similarly to the makerspace in a designated room, but they are mobile. You can think of these types of makerspaces as being popped-up and popped-out of the classroom or program. Materials can be organized by function and type and stored in rolling carts or boxes for easy transportation and storage. When setting up a pop-up makerspace, it is important to have a variety of materials so you can determine the most appropriate materials for each group of children.

> As Robin prepared a pop-up makerspace for Learn and Grow Child Care, she stocked the rolling carts with materials. She used the tables in the classroom to help define the space so the children could move about with ease. On the tables, she set up like objects, and she staged the building materials on the floor with plenty of space for measuring, cutting, and building. Robin placed two pairs of safety goggles in the building area to show how many children could be in the area at one time. Once introduced to the space, the children navigated their way to the various materials and began to engage.

> "When I had Tinker Tuesday in my classroom, I noticed that there were no behaviors that needed to be addressed. All the students were engaged and focused on their individual projects. Even the students that work collaboratively managed to stay on task. Tinker Tuesday was such a great experience, my students loved it!"
>
> —Nicole Cox, pre-K educator

SETTING THE STAGE FOR MAKERSPACE EXPERIENCES

Once you have set up your makerspace and chosen the materials, it is time to spur children's interest and establish expectations.

BUILDING EXCITEMENT

In the 1880s, if your community received the news that a traveling circus was coming to town, children would be full of anticipation and excitement. The anticipation children felt prior to the event enhanced the actual experience. Teachers can create anticipation and excitement by letting children know that a makerspace experience is coming to their classroom. There are several ways to do this, from simply asking questions to inspire thinking to posting signs in the room to offering clues to get the children guessing about what will be new in the classroom.

- Ask the children, "Do any of you like to use your imagination and make things?" Have the children describe what they have made in the past. With enthusiasm, ask, "Would you like to be makers and create something that only you can imagine?" Encourage the children to start thinking about things that they would be interested in making. Inform them that in X number of days they will have the opportunity to be makers.
- Make a sign that says "Coming Soon!" and post it on your classroom door. When students ask about the sign, you can reply in a mysterious voice that a makerspace is coming soon. Then ask the children what they think a maker-space might be. Encourage creative thoughts and ideas.
- Create several clues related to a makerspace. Tell the children that you are going to give them clues every day that week. The clues will give them ideas about an exciting new learning experience that they will have the following week, for example:

  o Clue 1: You will be able to use different types of tools, including an Allen wrench and a hand drill.
  o Clue 2: You can take apart an old computer, a calculator, and a video camera.
  o Clue 3: You can choose the materials you want to use, including bubble wrap, seedpods, aluminum foil, and wood blocks.
  o Clue 4: There will be only two rules.
  o Clue 5: You can work by yourself or with other children. You will be makers.

What are some other ideas that you could use to create anticipation and excitement about a makerspace experience?

INTRODUCING THE MAKERSPACE EXPERIENCE

You have created anticipation and excitement. The materials are set up in your space. Now it is time to introduce the makerspace experience to the children. Spark interest in a makerspace by reading a book related to making; invite the children to gather on a rug as you read a story.

> During a pop-up makerspace, Robin read the book *Be a Maker* by Katey Howes to a class of three-year-old children. As she read, she commented on the pictures and asked the children if they could recall a time when they made or created something at their home, in their class, or anywhere else. The children shared stories of some things they had created with their families and teachers.
>
> At the end of the story, Robin invited the children to "Be a Maker." She told them that they would have opportunities later that day to share their creations with the class. The only two directions she gave to the children were to be safe with the tools and have fun in making! The children moved to the different areas and began exploring the materials.

Using children's picture books related to making is a great way to introduce the concepts of tinkering, making, creating, exploring, and inventing. Books can spark children's imaginations and inspire their creative ideas. Within a makerspace, teachers can gain a greater understanding of what children are thinking and imagining. Books can also help to enhance the makerspace experience by introducing children to new vocabulary words and advanced language. As teachers read the books, they can ask intentional, open-ended questions designed to promote children's higher-level thinking skills. The concepts introduced within books help children make real-world connections. Books are also a great way to introduce storymaking and design challenges in makerspaces.

The following list of suggested books are great for introducing a makerspace, setting up a design challenge, prompting creative thinking, and inspiring creativity. Please keep in mind that this is not an all-inclusive list; it simply offers ideas on the types of books that would work well in connection with a makerspace in early childhood classrooms.

Children's Books to Introduce the Makerspace Experience

Alling, Niki. 2012. *When I Build with Blocks*. Scotts Valley, CA: CreateSpace.

> The everyday pre-K classroom is transported to a variety of places when young children play with blocks. Through a child's imagination, creating with blocks can take you from outer space to the ocean.

Beaty, Andrea. 2007. *Iggy Peck, Architect*. New York: Abrams Books for Young Readers.

> Iggy Peck loves to build things and solve problems, sometimes out of the strangest materials.

Beaty, Andrea. 2013. *Rosie Revere, Engineer*. New York: Abrams Books for Young Readers.

> Rosie wants to become an engineer. She builds great inventions from odds and ends and learns to celebrate failure and not give up.

Beaty, Andrea. 2016. *Ada Twist, Scientist*. New York: Abrams Books for Young Readers.

> Ada Twist is a born scientist—imaginative and curious. With the support of her family, Ada goes on fact-finding missions to answer the question why?

Bildner, Phil. 2004. *Twenty-One Elephants*. New York: Simon and Schuster.

> How many elephants will the newly constructed Brooklyn Bridge hold? Phineas T. Barnum decides to prove its strength.

Howes, Katey. 2019. *Be a Maker*. Minneapolis, MN: Carolrhoda Books.

> Take a journey of imagination with a little girl as she tries new things, discovers new ideas, and finds joy in making.

Portis, Antoinette. 2006. *Not a Box*. New York: HarperCollins.

> A small rabbit shows that a box will go as far as the imagination allows. Anything is possible with a cardboard box.

Portis, Antoinette. 2007. *Not a Stick*. New York: HarperCollins.

> A stick is not always just a stick. Imagination takes over when you give a child a stick.

Reynolds, Peter. 2003. *The Dot*. Somerville, MA: Candlewick.

> Vashti believes she is not an artist. One little dot on her paper takes her on a journey of surprise and self-discovery.

Ritchie, Scot. 2011. *Look at That Building! A First Book of Structures*. Toronto, ON: Kids Can Press.

> Five friends are going to build a doghouse, so they go to the library to learn about buildings and how they are constructed. Readers are invited to make their own mini doghouse.

Saltzberg, Barney. 2010. *Beautiful Oops!* New York: Workman.

> It is okay to make a mistake! Every mistake is an opportunity to make something beautiful. This is an encouraging story demonstrating the transformation from blunder to wonder.

Spires, Ashley. 2014. *The Most Magnificent Thing*. Toronto, ON: Kids Can Press.

> A little girl and her dog try to make the most magnificent thing. She fails at first, but with the help of her assistant, she finds that she can make the most magnificent thing.

VanDerwater, Amy Ludwig. 2018. *With My Hands*. Boston, MA: Clarion.

> Making something with your own hands is a special experience. This book invites the reader to tap into creativity and feel the energy that comes from making things.

SETTING BEHAVIORAL EXPECTATIONS FOR MAKERSPACES

As your makerspace starts to take shape, you will need to think about the behavioral expectations you will have for the children in the space and for the materials and tools. These expectations not only keep children safe but also encourage independence and the freedom to make choices. Whether it is a tinker tray, a pop-up, or an interest-center makerspace, similar behavioral expectations apply. These include making sure everyone has a turn, listening to others' ideas and opinions, respecting others' personal space and creations, using words to express emotions, asking for help when needed, and sharing in the task of cleaning up.

You will also need to determine how to ensure safety and classroom management. We suggest the following safety rules:

- Hand tools, such as a hammer, cardboard cutter, or hand drill, must be used with adult supervision.
- Eye protection, such as goggles, must be worn when using woodworking tools.
- Quickly report to an adult any broken tools, accidents, or issues.

It may be necessary to limit the number of children in the space, depending on the adult supervision required for specific activities. Modeling is an effective strategy for teaching these necessary rules.

We have found that children who are actively engaged in a makerspace experience rarely exhibit challenging behavior. Creating an environment that promotes active engagement takes thought and preparation. It is also important to have sufficient adult supervision available, especially during children's first makerspace experience.

Safety and fun are the two "rules" for children in a makerspace experience. As a teacher, you want children to be safe, and you also want them to have an enriching learning experience they will enjoy. With some thoughtful preparation, you can have both.

SUPERVISION

We recommend having a couple of extra adults present, such as program staff, administrators, or family volunteers. Designate one or more adults to help in the makerspace areas that require extra adult supervision, such as in the woodworking area. Take time to orient staff and volunteers on the expectations and the roles the adults are to play within a makerspace. Stress the importance of allowing children to take the lead in making. Emphasize that the adult's role is to be a supporter and encourager. Think about the specific children in your classroom and what individual needs they may have. Some children may need extra direction on using materials appropriately, and others may need a teacher close by to help them maintain their attention and focus.

Prepare the children as well by introducing them to unfamiliar tools and materials ahead of time and demonstrating how to safely use the tools prior to their first makerspace experience.

> Teacher Takisha plans to introduce a new tool, a rotary cutter, to the children for use in makerspace experiences. She sits on the rug with two to three children and talks with them about the tool, telling them how it works and showing how it cuts through different materials. She allows them to touch and explore the tool in a safe, controlled setting before allowing them to try cutting for themselves.

SPACE MANAGEMENT

Allow the children to freely move throughout the makerspace; however, in some areas, such as woodworking, that require additional supervision, it may be best to limit the number of children allowed in the space. Prior to the makerspace experience, inform the children of the number of children that can be in specific areas. For example, Sunny Days Preschool had only two sets of safety goggles available for use in the building-and-design area. When both pairs were in use, the area was "full" and children would have to wait until a pair of safety goggles was available before they could explore the area. In contrast, the other areas in the makerspace did not have a limit on the number of children who could explore and create.

TECHNOLOGY USE

Think about how technology will be used and monitored within the makerspace. Set rules and boundaries for use of items such as video cameras, a green screen, tablets, computers, and perhaps a 3-D printer. It is helpful if teachers demonstrate how to use the items. Make the expectations clear when you introduce the items. Show children how to safely operate and properly care for the technology. Remind children to take turns with the popular items and to be considerate of others. Some educators have found it helpful to create a sign-up sheet and set time limits to help manage turn taking for items that many children are interested in. If possible, have more than one of each item so children do not have to wait a long time for their turn. Technology can be a great addition to a makerspace; children can use it to document their processes and experiences through photos and video.

At Sunny Days Preschool, the director, Miss Kummaya, provided a few digital cameras for the children to use during their makerspace in the multipurpose room. She encouraged the children to use the cameras when they wanted to remember the creations they made. Trevor was so excited about using the camera that he took pictures of each of the children working around the room as well as all the materials he explored. Ms. Kummaya helped him see the pictures he took on the small screen, and then she printed out some of the pictures later while Trevor was eating lunch. Trevor was able to take a few of the pictures home to show his family the exciting activities from makerspace that day.

Using video cameras or tablets to record videos of the children encourages and supports storymaking and takes children's ideas and stories to the next level. Adding a green screen and digital apps that support animation and drawing lets technology bring to life what children imagine.

CLEANUP

Children need to know where to find materials and where materials and tools go when they are finished with them. Create a system so that everything has a designated space. It can be helpful to label containers with pictures and words to make cleaning up easier for everyone.

At Sunny Days Preschool, Ms. Maggie's class of four-year-old children entered the multipurpose room with anticipation about their chance to work in the makerspace. The teachers introduced the space, discussed the guidelines, and then watched the children actively engage in the materials for over an hour. Near the end of the time designated for the makerspace activity, Ms. Maggie let the children know that they would be transitioning to outside time soon. She pointed out the labels on the storage containers and asked for the children's help to put materials away in their places. She showed the children a designated table where they could put the items they create to save them for later or to take them home. All the children eagerly helped to clean up the areas they worked in, and there was little need for redirection because the storage containers were clearly labeled and accessible for the children.

 INTRODUCING THE MAKERSPACE

Once you have shared your expectations, invite the children to engage and freely explore and interact with the materials in the makerspace. After observing a pop-up makerspace, one of the facilitators shared the following insight: "I loved watching the children be unsure about having few rules and not being told what to do. They seemed hesitant at first, but when an adult didn't step in to give instructions, they began to be bold." Boldness and innovation are two of the key features of a makerspace experience. Children are empowered when they have time and space to create within a stimulating environment. Sometimes children need time to become familiar with and explore the materials before they are ready to become involved in making and creating.

> When Ms. Takisha introduced her four-year-old students to a makerspace in a designated room, she first allowed them to explore the different items and materials that were available. Children started touching, manipulating, and exploring the materials. With time, they were ready to start making and creating.

Children learn by watching others use materials and tools. Some of the materials in your makerspace may be unfamiliar to the children in your program, or they may not know how to effectively use the material. If you notice children are not using specific materials or tools, take time to model using the tools and materials. Observe whether your modeling impacts children's use of the materials and tools.

> When Charlee first introduced a makerspace using tinker trays in her classroom, she noticed some of the materials were not often chosen by the children. She wondered why the children were drawn to certain materials and not others. Some of the items that the children did not seem interested in at first were buttons, small wooden pieces, and tape. Charlee decided to do some modeling with the materials to see if the children would show more interest. She sat next to children who were stacking scraps of cardboard and began stacking the buttons and wooden pieces. Some of the children started mimicking her actions and were soon using the buttons in their tinkering.
>
> Charlee also modeled the use of the tape for the children. She demonstrated how to carefully peel the end of the tape up off the roll and how to use the scissors to cut the tape. The children began imitating her actions and developing their skills. They frequently asked Charlee to help them get the tape started. With additional time and support, the children became confident in using tape for their various creations and inventions.

 # MAINTAINING THE EXCITEMENT

As with any ongoing learning experience, it is important to maintain interest by adding variety and new elements over time. Children will benefit from having new challenges and opportunities to explore. Storymaking and design challenges are two ways to infuse and maintain excitement. The following list outlines the steps for facilitating a design challenge:

1. Select a book (or create a story problem) that poses a problem or challenge for the children to solve using the materials and tools in the makerspace.
2. Introduce the book (or story problem), and tell the children they will be brainstorming solutions and then selecting one of the ideas to try. Read the book (or story problem) to the children.
3. Guide the children in brainstorming solutions, and then have each child select a solution to try.
4. Invite the children to draw a plan for creating their solution. Support the children in drawing their plans.
5. Give the children time and space to create their solution using the materials and tools in the makerspace.
6. Have the children test their solutions and see if they are satisfied with the results. If not, discuss how they can adjust. Encourage the children to be persistent in creating a workable solution.

Here we offer several examples of how teachers have incorporated design challenges into their makerspaces.

Robin, the lead author, was providing coaching support to Ms. Takisha at Sunny Days Preschool. Once a week, Robin would observe Ms. Takisha's makerspace and then meet with her. They would talk about what went well, opportunities for improvement, and ways to maintain the excitement and interest in the makerspace.

During one of Robin's observations, she noticed that Ms. Takisha had put out the same creative-art materials for several weeks. The children were showing less engagement with the materials and having fewer animated conversations. Robin suggested that Ms. Takisha introduce a design challenge to re-engage and maintain excitement for makerspace. Using the information Robin gave her, Ms. Takisha thought about different types of design challenges she could have the children solve. She had been reading the book *If It Is Snowy and You Know It, Clap Your Paws!* by Kim Norman to the children recently. The children had been particularly interested in one of the illustrations in the book that featured several of the animals in an icy pond. Ms. Takisha used this area of interest to propose a problem for the children to solve. She challenged them to think of a way that they could rescue animals that fell through a hole in an icy pond.

After introducing the challenge, she asked the children to share their ideas. Their ideas included building bridges, creating a fishing rescue robot, and rescuing the animals with a submarine. After brainstorming, Ms. Takisha encouraged each child to draw out a plan for how to rescue the animals. Once their plans were drawn, she invited the children to create their solutions using the materials and tools in the makerspace. Ms. Takisha supported the children as they brought their plans to life and created their rescue items.

During the design challenge, Irik told Ms. Takisha that he was going to build a robot submarine to help the animals get out of the cold water and get home. Ms. Takisha asked Irik to think about how he would make the robot submarine, what materials he would need, and how he would assemble the parts. Irik drew his plan, or blueprint, for the robot submarine, then he said that he needed fins for the sides and long pieces for the body. He gathered the materials and began to execute his plan, making sure that the materials lined up just as he had drawn on his blueprint. Once completed, he compared his robot submarine to the one he planned and was satisfied with the results.

At Learn and Grow Child Care, Charlee noticed that the children were less engaged in the makerspace than they had been previously. During coaching, Robin asked Charlee why she thought this was so. Charlee replied that she thought the children were tired of the materials and needed new materials and tools. Robin and Charlee spoke about the times when the children were most engaged and how to regain and maintain the excitement. Robin suggested adding either storymaking or a design challenge to reignite the spark. Charlee liked the idea of a design challenge, and together Robin and Charlee created a plan for the week using the book *Twenty-One Elephants* by Phil Bildner.

Charlee highlighted several pages from the story and then challenged the children to create a bridge that twenty-one elephants could walk over. She showed the children pictures of different types of bridges. She asked them to brainstorm different types of materials they could use to create a bridge. Charlee told the children they could work together or independently. The children were encouraged to draw out their plans and then use the materials in the makerspace to create their planned bridges. The children quickly got to work creating bridges with items such as cardboard tubes, foam, and wooden sticks. Next, they tested them with plastic toy animals.

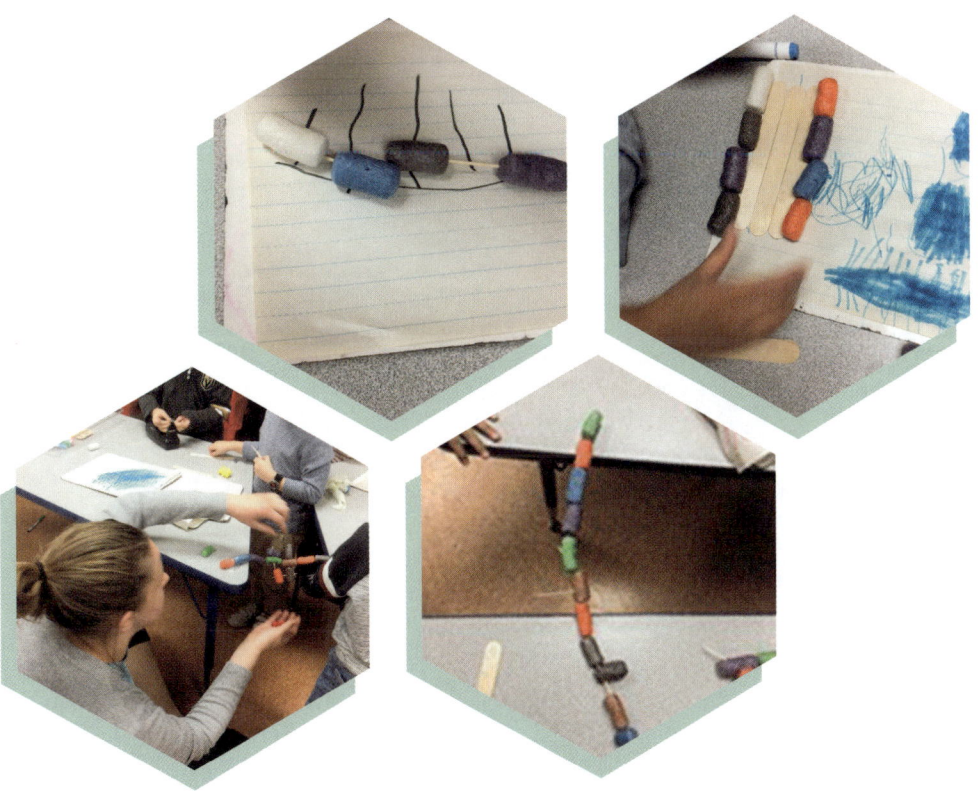

You now have a blueprint for setting up the makerspace, introducing children to the makerspace experiences, establishing expectations, and maintaining children's excitement for the makerspace. In the next chapter, we describe many of the skills children develop while engaged in a makerspace.

5 BUILDING SKILLS

Makerspace experiences provide children with opportunities to develop skills in all of the developmental domains, including cognitive thinking, social-emotional skills, and motor skills. Engaging in makerspace experiences naturally enhances children's maker mindsets and encourages them to create what they imagine. In doing so, they build skills they'll use in the future, foster their natural curiosity, increase their engagement and attention span, and learn how to collaborate with others.

 ## DEVELOPING CHILDREN'S COGNITIVE SKILLS

Cognitive development is a broad term that encompasses thinking, intelligence, and language abilities. Children develop these skills as they grow, adapt, and change in response to meaningful, authentic experiences. As children gain more experience in the world and come to understand more complex concepts, their cognitive development is enhanced.

According to Sylvia Martinez and Gary Stager, authors of *Invent to Learn*, "when we allow children to experiment, take risks, and play with their own ideas, we give them permission to trust themselves." This helps children begin to see themselves as learners who have good ideas and can transform their own ideas into reality.

While in the makerspace interest center, five-year-old Clayton is sharing a recipe for a "bean cake." He explains to Ryan and Alida what ingredients they will need to create their own cakes. As Ryan and Alida work on their cakes, they exercise cognitive skills in subjects such as science and math; physical skills through fine-motor development; and social and emotional skills as they take turns, listen to each other, share materials, and work collaboratively. These children are building language and literacy skills as they dictate to their teacher, Ms. Jones, the ingredients they will be using and create a recipe for future reference.

Cognitive skills children build while engaging in makerspaces include the following:

- Convergent and divergent thinking
- Experimenting, risk taking, and playing with their own ideas
- Problem solving
- Discovering the properties of objects
- Classification, measurement, balance, and conservation
- Imaginative thinking and expression of ideas and emotions
- Understanding symbolic representation

Convergent and Divergent Thinking

Convergent thinking is the ability to give the one correct answer to a problem. In contrast, *divergent thinking* is the ability to think of multiple ideas or solutions to a problem. Divergent thinking is similar to brainstorming lots of ideas and requires a higher level of creativity. As children engage with materials in a makerspace, it becomes evident that both convergent and divergent thinking are present.

Materials that encourage convergent thinking are those that can be used to arrive at one correct solution. According to author Fergus Hughes, "materials that encourage divergent thinking are those that do not lead to one correct solution but instead offer a range of possibilities for their use." Makerspace materials can prompt divergent problem solving. We have observed children looking at a common problem and then coming up with several unique solutions. When discussing divergent problem solving in his article in the *Creative Research Journal*, Arthur Cropley writes, "It is the ability to branch out from a starting point and consider a variety of possible solutions." Both convergent thinking and divergent thinking have value. Divergent thinking is especially involved in the creative process. Findings in a study by Kara Gregory, An Sook Kim, and Alice Whiren indicate that children benefit most when they have many opportunities to explore materials and are supported by a caring adult engaged in verbal scaffolding during the learning process.

PROBLEM SOLVING AND COGNITIVE DEVELOPMENT

Psychologists have discovered that there is a relationship between children's problem-solving approaches and the characteristics of their play materials. Consider the findings of a classic study by researchers Debra Pepler and Hildy Ross, who gave sixty-four preschool children the opportunity to play with either convergent materials, such as puzzles with one correct solution, or divergent materials, such as blocks, which can be assembled in a variety of ways. They divided the children into two groups and repeatedly presented them with one type of material (either convergent or divergent) for play. Later, they asked the children in the two groups to solve a variety of problems. When the researchers examined the children's problem-solving approaches, those who had engaged in divergent object play were more flexible and more original in their problem solving than the group that engaged in convergent materials. Arthur Cropley stated, "They were quicker than those in the convergent group to abandon ineffective approaches to solving problems and to come up with new approaches."

According to researcher Olivia Saracho, "When children are involved in environments rich in play materials that include a variety of options in the use of the materials, the learning experience facilitates children's divergent thinking and generates a creative mindset." This type of environment matches the concept of makerspace experiences, which offer children a variety of options and allow them to use materials in creative ways.

LANGUAGE AND LITERACY SKILLS
AND COGNITIVE DEVELOPMENT

A makerspace provides a golden opportunity to ask open-ended questions and spark conversations about what children plan, observe, and execute. As children collaborate building a high-rise tower out of cardboard, they engage in two-way conversations by taking turns listening and speaking. Children develop expressive language skills as they retell a story or describe how they used the hand drill in the woodworking area. Makerspaces also afford teachers the opportunity to introduce and define new and challenging vocabulary words. The use of pictures and makerspace materials help children make connections with new words. Access to a variety of writing materials and tools such as clipboards, journals, graph paper, markers, and pencils encourage children to become proficient at writing words and sentences. Language development is more than just communication; it is about making connections and building relationships.

During a makerspace experience at Learn and Grow Child Care, Ms. Holly is at the natural-materials table having a back-and-forth exchange with Andrew. Ms. Holly speaks English, and Andrew speaks only Mandarin but understands some English. Andrew is manipulating a tray containing clear, flat glass beads; one clear, round marble; and some tree disks. Andrew notices that the marble moves around the tray and that nothing else on the tray moves. He looks up to Ms. Holly, and she asks him, "Why do you think the marble is moving?" as she points to the marble and makes a moving motion with her finger. Andrew does not verbally respond; he looks at Ms. Holly and holds up the marble. Ms. Holly says it is a marble and is round like a ball. She draws a round shape in the air to convey to Andrew that the marble is round and will roll on the tray. She then holds up a glass bead and uses motions to tell Andrew that the bead is flat. She shows him the two objects side by side.

Andrew takes the round marble and flat beads and places them on the tray, then he arranges the tree disks on the tray. Andrew picks up the tray and starts moving it back and forth from side to side. "Wow, Andrew!" Ms. Holly exclaims, "The marble is rolling in between the tree disks. You created a marble maze." Ms. Holly points at the tree disks and asks Andrew if he wants to move the tree disks into a different pattern. Andrew rearranges the tree disks, removing some of them from the tray, along with the glass beads. Andrew continues creating marble mazes until he decides to move on to a different area.

This is an example of a teacher using verbal and nonverbal communication to support a dual language learner. Her interest and attention in Andrew's making strengthened her connection with him and built their relationship.

Teachers play an important role in modeling behaviors. During one observation of Ms. Nikki, Robin walked into the classroom and overheard the following conversation between preschoolers Kyle and Hunter:

> Kyle, holding a clipboard, stands close to Hunter and says, "Tell me what you are going to create today. What materials will you use?" Kyle "documents" Hunter's reply on the clipboard. Ms. Nikki, the teacher, looks at Robin with a sense of pride. It is fulfilling for Ms. Nikki to hear Kyle ask Hunter some of the same open-ended questions that she has asked children during their classroom makerspace experience.
>
> The children were so familiar with the questions asked by Ms. Nikki that they began asking them to their peers and "documenting" their answers. Never underestimate the power of modeling.

Mathematics Skills and Cognitive Development

As children engage with makerspace materials, they discover the properties of objects and learn skills, such as classification, measurement, balance, and conservation, on their own. Even simple interactions with makerspace materials can prompt new skill development and provide opportunities to construct concepts at the child's pace.

> In a makerspace interest center, Mr. Austin notices four-year-old James trying to devise a way to build a bridge across two rivers he has drawn. Austin watches as James locates a container of craft sticks and begins laying the sticks on his paper. James measures the length of the bridge by comparing it to the drawing on the paper. As he places the sticks on the paper, they move out of place. James looks up and makes eye contact with his teacher. Austin says, "I notice you are looking for a solution to stop the sticks from moving. I wonder what you could do to help secure them." James moves around the room looking at other makerspace materials and then picks up a glue bottle. James puts glue on some additional craft sticks and places them as cross pieces to connect the sticks together. Austin says, "I see you've thought of a solution."

Creative Arts and Cognitive Development

Using different materials within a makerspace can evoke children's imaginative thinking and the expression of their ideas and emotions. As children engage with these materials, they have opportunities for enhanced cognitive development, developing their understanding of symbolic representation, and creativity. Children can reflect on their own thinking and engage in complex thought processes. They have opportunities to enhance their *visual literacy*, which is the ability to make meaning through visual images, as seen in the following example.

> Lilianna and William discover a variety of rocks, gems, buttons, and foam packing material on a makerspace tinker tray. Using drawing paper on clipboards, they draw representations of each item. Lilianna and William are developing two key abilities: symbolic representation and visual literacy, which support language and literacy as well as thinking in all areas.

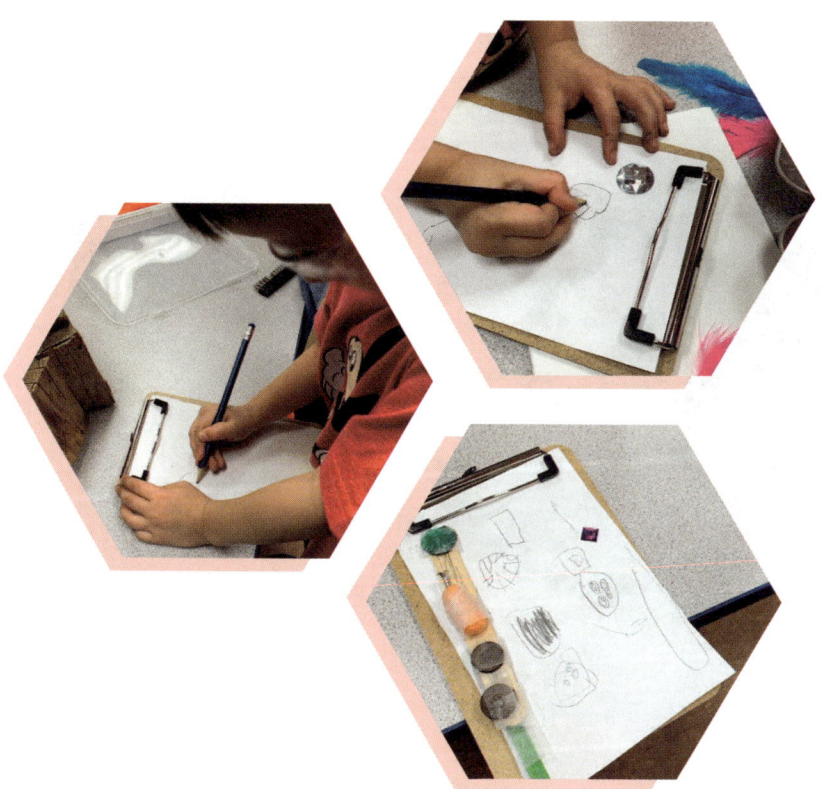

SOCIAL-EMOTIONAL DEVELOPMENT

According to researcher and educator Sunil Batra, "At the heart of every school-based relationship, whether with peers, teachers, books, or the physical space that students inhabit, lies the social and emotional development of all children, an often unrecognized and unappreciated aspect of human development." Erik Erikson, a psychologist best known for his theory of psychosocial development, notes, "Children between the ages of three and six years are learning to imagine, they are becoming more independent, and they are learning to cooperate with others."

Children develop many social-emotional skills during the first six years of life. According to The Center on the Social and Emotional Foundations for Early Learning, "Children are learning many important social emotional skills that include confidence, relationships with peers and adults, concentration, and persistence. These skills are needed throughout life. Children are also learning to communicate their emotions and to listen attentively. When children lack these skills, they are more likely to exhibit challenging behaviors. Therefore, it is essential that children are taught social-emotional skills during the early years."

Social-Emotional Skills

Children can learn a number of social-emotional skills during makerspace experiences. They develop a sense of independence by deciding what items to explore and determining what materials they will use to make and create. Children have opportunities to share items, work independently and cooperatively, as well as watch and learn from each other. The following example shows how children can gain confidence and learn new things by observing their peers.

Joel is hesitant to explore and tinker. He walks around the room and then stops when he notices the electronics. He approaches the table and stands very close to Zayne, who is exploring the inside of a computer. Zayne continues exploring the computer as Joel looks on. After a few minutes of observing, Joel begins to take items from the table and to explore some of the electronics himself.

Within a makerspace, children have opportunities to work both independently and collaboratively. These experiences support the development of their communication skills and their ability to cooperate. (We will discuss collaboration in more depth on page 85.)

Brayden, Denym, and Kamdyn are talking about monsters and how to trap them. They tell their teacher, Ms. Maggie, that they want to build a house to trap some monsters. Ms. Maggie asks them what materials they will need. Brayden tells her that they need a house, so she asks him how he can make a house with the materials on the table. Denym says that they can use a box, and Kamdyn suggests that they use tape to close the doors, so the monsters do not get out. Working cooperatively, the boys use the materials on the table to secure the box and then negotiate how to integrate their ideas until they finish the house.

Social-emotional skills children build while engaging in a makerspace include:

- Working independently
- Working collaboratively
- Building relationships
- Cooperating
- Expressing ideas
- Problem solving
- Communicating
- Attending to tasks

PHYSICAL DEVELOPMENT

Young children develop physical skills, including gross-motor (large-muscle) skill development and fine-motor (small-muscle) skill development, at a rapid pace during the first five years of life. Children develop gross-motor skills as they walk, run, balance, coordinate large body movements, and manipulate heavy objects. Fine-motor skills develop as children pick up and hold small objects, cut, thread, and coordinate hand

and eye movements as they manipulate objects. Children need a variety of experiences to develop their physical skills.

Early childhood educators can promote children's physical development by providing preschoolers with multiple opportunities to use their large and small muscles. Children's mastery of different physical skills builds their self-esteem and gives them confidence to try new things. Active, creative, and playful exploration can reduce stress and lead to improved academic learning. Providing a variety of activities for children to develop their large and small muscles within a makerspace encourages children to engage in physical development activities while allowing them to make choices and build their confidence and skills.

Gross-Motor Skills

A great thing about allowing children to explore and learn in a makerspace is that children can make choices and develop their skills by doing what interests them. During one makerspace experience, Sarah, one of the authors, observed a group of children exploring large cardboard boxes.

Jordon stands up on his tiptoes and uses his large muscles to pick up a box as big as his torso and move it onto the floor. Jordon and his friend Sam begin using scissors to cut off parts of the cardboard. Sam holds up one long piece that touches the floor and says, "I am making a snowboard." Jordon and a few other children look up with interest as Sam lays the cardboard strip on the floor and places both feet on top of it. He holds out his arms to his side and says, "Look at me on the snowboard!" Several other children quickly hurry over to Sam, and Carlos asks if he can have a turn. Sam steps off the snowboard he created and allows Carlos to step on. Carlos holds out his arms as Sam has just done and then lifts one foot off the ground. He balances for a moment and then looks at Sam and laughs. Their large muscle development is evident as they demonstrate strength, balance, coordination, and muscle control.

Fine-Motor Skills

While Sam, Jordon, and Carlos were making their snowboards, a different group of children in the same room were using a variety of materials and developing their fine-motor skills.

Preschool teacher Samantha has placed hole punches, paper-towel tubes, and scissors on a table in her classroom. She shows the children how to use the hole punchers and then encourages them to use the tools on their own. At first, several of the children struggle, but after a while, the children gain confidence and punch holes in the paper-towel tubes independently.

Liam, a three-year-old, and Brody, a four-year-old, test the differences in the hole punchers by punching holes into their tubes. Soon Brody announces that he likes the hole puncher with the black handle the best and asks Liam to trade with him. "Okay," Liam says. "The big hole puncher works better on this tube." Liam punches a hole into the top of a paper-towel roll and carefully pokes the tip of a piece of yarn into the hole. Liam looks at his teacher, Charlee, and announces, "I want to build a bridge, like the book." Charlee had read the children a book about bridges earlier in the day, and it seems that Liam feels inspired.

A small group of children work together and share materials to build a bridge between two tables. Brody holds one tube in each hand and steadies them on a table while Liam holds two other tubes on a nearby table. The boys make eye contact and let go of the tubes they are holding at the same time. The bridge falls down off the tables, and Brody and Liam let out a gasp. Charlee approaches the boys and asks, "What happened?" Liam explains that the bridge they are building is not staying up, so Charlee asks, "What do you think we could do to solve this problem?"

"Maybe we can use the blue tape!" Brody responds excitedly.

"What a great idea," Charlee says. "Can you go get the tape from the art center so you can try out your solution?" Brody and Liam run to get the tape and bring it back to where they are building a bridge.

Pointing at the tube, Brody directs, "Liam, you hold it, and I will tape it to the table." Brody uses his fine-motor skills to peel and tear each piece of tape as the boys work together to make the bridge stand on its own.

Meanwhile, Erika is trying to use scissors to cut a paper-towel roll. She is having some difficulty holding the scissors and making them cut. An adult volunteer, Lori, observes her holding the scissors and identifies that Erika needs extra support with her fine-motor skills. Lori approaches Erika, gets down at her level, smiles, and says, "Tell me about what you are doing."

Erika looks at Lori and responds, "Cutting." As Lori sits near Erika and talks with her, she gives Erika some verbal instructions about how she can turn the scissors around in her hand to be more successful in cutting. During the next few days, Lori continues to support Erika by giving her more opportunities to practice cutting different materials. This is helping Erika develop her fine-motor skills in a variety of ways. Erika quickly develops confidence and fine motor skills as she engages in activities such as cutting and stringing beads together to make a bracelet.

There is no limit to the skills children can practice as they manipulate materials, move in new ways, and let their creativity expand. Fine-motor skills children build while engaging in makerspaces include:

- Using scissors to cut
- Turning a screwdriver
- Threading yarn, ribbon, or string
- Folding paper
- Holding a golf tee steady to hammer it
- Peeling tape
- Moving and sorting small materials
- Marking measurements with a pencil
- Tying knots
- Pinching tweezers, clothes pins, or tongs

Gross-motor skills children build while engaging in makerspaces include:

- Balancing on tiptoes to reach for something
- Stretching to measure a large item

- Bending, crouching, and coordinating movements
- Lifting and carrying large materials
- Crawling into a newly formed tunnel
- Navigating space around people and materials

Children in a makerspace are frequently standing, reaching, crouching, and lifting both large and small materials. The following story is an example of how children will use materials in new ways when given the time to be creative.

One morning, Gina, a teacher in a preschool classroom, sets out ribbon and other materials on a tinker tray. The children in Gina's class have the freedom to tinker and create whatever they want with the available materials. Jeremy, a three-year-old child, decides to hold some colorful ribbons and walks around the class with the ribbons trailing behind him. He begins to wrap the ribbons around the chairs that are set up around the table. Soon there is an obstacle course set up entirely from Jeremy's creativity and exploration of the material. The other children quickly become interested in what Jeremy has made. With Gina carefully monitoring the activity, some children choose to step over or crawl under the ribbons. These children are exercising their large muscles while building skills and confidence. They encourage each other as they move through the obstacle course. Gina observes and documents the children's abilities to balance, take turns, and create their own rules for the activity they invented.

⚙️⚙️ DEVELOPING LIFE SKILLS ⚙️⚙️

Children become and stay engaged when they are interested in what they are doing. Young children are naturally curious about how things work. They enjoy exploring different materials and discovering more about the world that they live in. Makerspace experiences are designed to involve children in the act of being creative as they tinker and invent. According to Janette Hughes, a researcher at the University of Ontario Institute of Technology, "Students in a makerspace environment are more engaged and motivated to learn. Additionally, these students exhibit less challenging behavior. In a makerspace, children are allowed to wonder and act upon their wonderings. Children create their own meaningful and authentic learning experiences. They are learning twenty-first century skills, such as collaboration and perseverance." In makerspaces, children build skills they'll use in the future as they engage their curiosity, increase their engagement and attention span, and collaborate with peers.

SKILLS FOR THE FUTURE

When early childhood programs embrace makerspaces, a culture of innovation and creativity begins to flourish. Children learn from their mistakes and become more comfortable with risk taking and engaging in trial and error. They learn how to persevere and gain confidence to keep going by trying different ideas and solutions. Children enjoy making things by using both their hands and their minds.

According to Sylvia Martinez and Gary Stager, authors of *Invent to Learn*, when we allow children to experiment, take risks, and play with their own ideas, we give them permission to trust themselves. They begin to see themselves as learners who have good ideas and can transform their own ideas into reality. Makerspace experiences are designed to prepare students for the future. Businesses value skills such as creativity, perseverance, problem solving, collaboration, sustained attention, and the ability to use higher-order thinking skills.

As the world rapidly changes and as advances in technology create new fields of work, these skills will continue to be important.

Additionally, makerspaces are learning environments that are ideal for children who struggle within very structured learning environments. The flexible nature of the maker-space offers children the opportunity for interdisciplinary learning. They can progress at their own pace and through their own personal method of learning. In fact, the makerspace environment is closely matched to how the real world works. Concepts are not taught in isolation; instead, ideas are learned through an integrated approach. This type of education is a more realistic approach to life and learning.

CURIOSITY

Children are especially curious when they have opportunities to interact with intriguing materials and tools. Children's imaginations are stimulated by novelty—and positive surprises can promote children's curiosity. Through exploration and trial and error, children learn more about the world. Their curiosity drives them to find answers to their questions. Teachers can nurture this curiosity and involve children in expressing their thoughts and ideas by asking open-ended questions:

- "What do you think will happen if. . ."
- "Why do you think that happened?"
- "What do you think you can do to solve that problem?"

Open-ended questions can encourage children to discuss what they are experiencing and can spark creativity. For a more comprehensive list of these questions, see page 99.

Fred looks at the materials that Veronica, his teacher, has placed on the table for the day's makerspace. He picks up a paper-towel tube and a roll of tape. "Ms. Roni," he asks, "can I tape these over there on the wall?"

"Sure," says Veronica. "What's your plan with those materials?"

Fred replies, "I dunno."

Fred and Veronica begin taping tubes to the wall in various directions. As Fred looks at the tubes on the wall, Veronica asks, "Should we see what would happen if we dropped something into the top of the tubes?"

"Yeah!" exclaims Fred. He runs to the makerspace table and picks out three large pompoms. Fred smiles a wide smile and says, "Two, one, go," as he drops an orange pompom down the first tube. The pompom rolls out of the tube and into another tube. Fred shrieks and jumps up and down. He quickly grabs the next pompom and places it in the tube again. This time, the pompom falls to the ground. "How did I make it go into this one?" Fred asks, pointing at the second tube.

"That is a mystery," replies Veronica. "What do you think happened?" Fred continues to drop pompoms into the tubes over and over again, because he is so curious about how his invention works.

ENGAGEMENT AND ATTENTION SPAN

Teachers we have worked with have noticed a difference in their children's engagement when they participate in a makerspace experience. One teacher shared, "I took my class to the makerspace room. What I noticed through this activity was ALL of the children were engaged in one of the areas. I also noticed there were no issues with challenging behavior. There were many things set up in the makerspace that you would not normally see in typical classrooms, and that opened up the world of creativity and imagination for the children."

Children in makerspace environments often demonstrate high engagement and sustained attention. *Sustained attention* is the ability to maintain attention on a task over an extended period of time. A child's typical attention span is about 3 to 5 minutes per year of age; four-year-olds are generally able to maintain attention for 12 to 20 minutes. When children are engaged in an interesting task, however, they frequently exhibit sustained attention for a longer period.

Anthony and Enrique are two active boys in Ms. Takisha's preschool classroom. They rarely sit still for more than 5 minutes; they are usually busy touching and exploring the environment. One day, Takisha sets out makerspace materials that include natural playdough, twigs, leaves, seashells, and other natural materials. Anthony and Enrique go over to the space and start to create. Takisha is amazed as 15 minutes, then 40 minutes, and finally 1 hour and 10 minutes go by and Anthony and Enrique are *still* interacting with the materials. The boys create cookies and imaginary characters with the materials that have captivated their interest and imagination.

COLLABORATION

Another important life skill is *collaboration*—working with others to produce or create something or to achieve a goal. Collaboration requires children to think more deeply about ideas, communicate clearly, and solve problems together, which are team-building skills. According to a survey conducted on behalf of the Association of American Colleges and Universities (2018), 81 percent of employers in midsize to large companies list collaboration skills as desired attributes in the individuals they want to hire. In makerspaces such as the one in Maria's preschool class, young children have opportunities to develop these skills.

The children in teacher Maria's preschool class have been learning about bears and hibernation. Maria plans to divide the children into two groups and give them a design challenge to create a cave in which bears can hibernate during the winter. The children have access to a wide variety of materials, including large cardboard boxes, tubes, brown paper, and lots of tape.

"Good morning, children," says Maria. "Today, you are going to have the opportunity to create a cave for a bear family to hibernate in. I am going to place you into two teams, and I want you to work together using any of these materials to create your cave. First, you should talk with your team about what you want to include in your cave, and then you will work together to create your cave. Any questions?"

The children form their two groups and begin to talk about what they want to include in their caves. In the first group, Michael says, "I think the bears will need a big cave."

Andrew responds, "Yes! They'll all need places to sleep." The children start to construct their cave.

"I know!" says Iris excitedly, "Let's build a bunk bed for the bear cubs to sleep on."

"How could we do that?" asks Mario. The children try several different ideas until they figure out a way to tape brown paper to the top of the box so that it forms a pocket that will act as the baby-bear bunk bed.

"They need a pillow and a blanket," says Amber.

"I'll help you make them," says Sam.

As the cave progresses, Michael is concerned that the baby bears do not have anything fun to do. "What if we make the baby bears a slide?" he asks.

"Yeah," says Mario, "a slide would be cool."

"Let's put it on the roof," suggests Erin. The children actively work on creating a baby-bear slide on the roof of their cave.

Meanwhile, the second group is working on their cave. Zelda says, "I think the bears need a garage and a garage-door opener."

"I want to make a tunnel so the bears can go into the cave," says Marco. He goes to find some supplies to make a tunnel.

"I can help hold the tape," offers Jackson.

"Make sure you tape it down good," says Liz.

"What if Santa wants to bring the bears presents?" asks Jamie.

"Let's make a chimney so Santa can come in," says Liz.

"Here's a long tube—would that work?" asks Liam. The children work together to create a chimney for Santa.

When the caves are completed, the children eagerly share what they each worked on to create their caves. "I added bear ears to our cave, so the bears know they can go in." says Erin.

"I made a mailbox so the bears can get letters," says Michael.

"I made a lookout so the bears can see who is coming," says Marco.

"You all did a great job of working together to create your bear caves," says Maria. "I love how you collaborated and worked cooperatively with your group."

In this chapter, we saw how children develop cognitive, social-emotional, and physical skills within makerspace experiences. They learn how to collaborate and persevere as they engage in problem solving and use their imagination. This innovative environment sparks their curiosity, fosters their engagement, and helps children learn essential twenty-first century life skills. In the next chapter, we'll look at the teacher's role in creating the optimal makerspace experience for young children.

6

THE TEACHER'S ROLE

Have you read the children's folktale *Caps for Sale* by Esphyr Slobodkina? It is a story of a peddler who has a stack of caps in a variety of colors on his head. He carefully balances the caps as he walks through the streets, calling, "Caps for sale!" Teachers of young children often relate to this story because they too wear many "caps"—assuming different roles throughout the day as they provide quality learning experiences. This chapter explores what each of these roles would look like in a makerspace experience.

 ## THE MANY CAPS TEACHERS WEAR IN MAKERSPACES

Some of the caps teachers wear include planner, facilitator, observer, guide, role model, and questioner. All of these roles are important to young children's development.

PLANNER

One of the caps teachers wear is the cap of planner. They plan how they will meet specific learning objectives and how they will deliver engaging educational experiences to young children. Within the context of a makerspace, teachers ask themselves questions such as, "What is the goal of this makerspace?" "What materials does my school already have?" "How much physical space do I have available for a makerspace?" Teachers evaluate their classroom space based on the children's perspective. They identify maker materials, keeping in mind children's cultures, languages, and differing abilities. They determine how to display the materials and equipment in a makerspace, so that children will be stimulated, interested, and challenged. Teachers plan how to be flexible and prepare to adapt and rearrange materials and tools to provide the most enriching learning experiences for all children, as seen in the following example.

> Alexa, a three-year-old child with an identified intellectual disability, enjoyed exploring the materials on the tinker trays during makerspace. She approached the materials excitedly and seemed to enjoy their colors and textures. Her favorite material was the ribbons. She unrolled the ribbons from the spool and tossed a handful above her head. Lifting her face toward the ceiling, she smiled widely as they drifted down and brushed her cheeks. She enjoyed tossing them over and over again. Alexa's teacher, Charlee, noticed this interest and planned to include the colorful ribbons for Alexa to explore during their next makerspace experiences.

FACILITATOR

As children move into the makerspace, a teacher's role shifts to wearing the facilitator cap. Facilitators offer support and scaffold children's learning experiences. They build on children's current knowledge base and help them find their own answers to questions. As the facilitator, teachers are available to the children. They observe and listen as children engage with the makerspace materials and watch for children's moments of discovery, ready to prompt as needed with an open-ended question. They urge children to consider "what if?"

In the makerspace, the teacher facilitator gives up some of the control that often accompanies being a teacher. As illustrated in the *Caps for Sale* folktale, the peddler spends a great deal of time practicing the art of balancing all his caps on his head. Likewise, teachers may find that giving up some of their control may take some practice, but it is well worth the effort. The facilitator understands that a child's learning will be less meaningful if he is given all the answers. The facilitator does not want to disrupt children's learning during their road to discovery. Teachers must resist the urge to step in and take over an activity when they see a child struggling. Instead, hold onto your caps and allow children to problem solve and discover the solution for themselves.

OBSERVER

Observers focus on the actions of children to gain insights about what they are doing, how they are developing, and what skills they are learning. When teachers wear the observer cap, they pay particular attention to children's strengths and opportunities for growth. It is through the role of observer that a teacher will begin to see which skills a child has mastered and which skills may need additional support. The observer also becomes more aware of a child's linguistic and developmental needs.

In a makerspace, the observer will pause, tune into the moment, and take note of a child's heightened interest or lack of interest. The role of observer provides a way for teachers to gain greater understanding about each child. Observation helps teachers think of ways to connect with each child and strengthen their relationships.

During his first pop-up makerspace experience, four-year-old Alex became very interested in an older video camera, which had been donated to the program. Sarah, one of the authors, observed Alex as he thoroughly inspected the camera, turning it around in his hands and pushing every button.

Alex told Sarah he was going to fix the camera so he could use it to make a movie. Sarah asked him to tell her more about what he was going to do. Alex said he would need tools, so they walked together over to the table with the tools. He scanned the different items on the table and picked up a pair of pliers. He tried fitting them in each opening of the camera but quickly decided the pliers were not the correct tool for the repairs. He set the pliers down on the table and looked over the tools again. Another child, Brian, was standing close by and asked Alex what he was doing. "Finding a tool," Alex answered.

Brian looked at the tools laid out on the table and picked up the hammer. He told Alex, "This hammer is for pounding." Alex shook his head no. Brian picked up another tool and asked, "How about a screwdriver?" Alex looked at the screwdriver for a few moments and then replied, "Yeah, let me see it." Alex took the screwdriver in his fist and carefully matched it up to an exposed screw on the camera.

He quickly noticed the screwdriver was too big to fit into the head of the screw. He tried the screwdriver on every screw he could see. His focus was fully on the camera as he tested each screw. Sarah quietly observed him and noticed his determination to find a screw he could turn with the screwdriver. After trying each screw, he looked up at Sarah and said, "I think I need a smaller screwdriver." He asked Sarah to bring a "baby" screwdriver the next time she visited his school. He even told her to write it down so she would not forget. Sarah wrote herself a note to bring a small screwdriver.

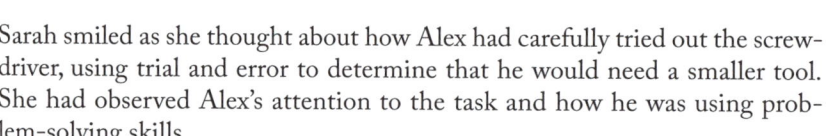

Sarah smiled as she thought about how Alex had carefully tried out the screwdriver, using trial and error to determine that he would need a smaller tool. She had observed Alex's attention to the task and how he was using problem-solving skills.

Alex spent another 30 minutes using the screwdriver to try to fix the video camera. Sarah thought about how Alex would benefit from additional hands-on experiences that required him to problem solve. She also noted that Alex had an interest in making a movie.

This example illustrates the valuable information teachers can glean when they wear their observer cap. By paying attention to children's emerging interests, teachers are able to plan learning experiences that are meaningful for each child.

GUIDE

A guide is someone who shows the way, often leading others down new paths. They frequently walk beside a person, giving pertinent information. They are often enthusiastic about what they can show and tell others. Guides give individuals freedom to explore and have new experiences. They also keep the people in their care safe from harm. According to Jill Miels, author of "The Seven Faces of the Early Childhood Educator," teachers should function as guides, rather than dispensers of knowledge, for the children in their care. When teachers wear the cap of a guide, they show children the way and then allow them to explore, giving children opportunities to choose how they will play and learn.

Guides are essential for a child's successful makerspace experience. They ensure the makerspace experience is fluid and easy to navigate, with few barriers. They are available to offer suggestions about materials and tools, but they allow children to take the lead in making their own choices. Guides know the landscape and relish in helping others discover the richness and beauty that it offers. They are familiar with the path and are prepared. As a guide, you can help children have their best adventure.

A group of three-year-old children at Learn and Grow Child Care walk hesitantly from their classroom into the room next door where the pop-up makerspace is set up. It is their first time experiencing a makerspace, and they huddle together close to their teacher. Ms. Sang announces the different types of makerspace materials children can explore. She says, "You are invited to explore the materials and tools on each of the tables." She then guides the children to another part of the room and tells them about the items they can explore on the carpet, such as cardboard tubes, a basket of balls and pompoms, paper-towel holders, napkin rings, brush curlers, and plastic cups. She also shows them a space for using tools and building. The children seem especially excited to try using the hammer and manual drill. Ms. Sang tells them that the number of children using tools at one time will be limited to four, so that everyone will stay safe. As interest in the area is high, Ms. Sang shows the children that there are tools in other areas. She points to the technology area and says, "I see some different tools over there. Let's go check it out." Her gentle guidance prompts several of the children to move to the technology area.

Part of the role of the guide is to act as an encourager and prompt children to try new experiences. This allows children to build their confidence as they explore unfamiliar materials and tools. As you guide them in a makerspace experience, be enthusiastic about children's discoveries, celebrate their achievements, and encourage them when they struggle. Children learn a lot when they are encouraged to be persistent and to keep trying, especially when things are not working out as planned. Encouragement is most meaningful when you give specific feedback: "Taylor, you kept trying different ideas until you solved the problem. You are a persistent problem solver." Statements such as this one help children to see the value of not giving up. Teachers can support children in many ways by acting as guides during makerspace experiences.

Danica, a four-year-old child diagnosed with autism spectrum disorder, was hesitant to approach the materials set out for the makerspace in the multipurpose room. Knowing that Danica was very interested in bugs, her teacher, Gigi, had intentionally set out some plastic bugs along with the natural playdough, sticks, pinecones, and leaves. Gigi said, "Look, Danica, there are bugs on the table," as she gently guided her to space. Danica carefully picked up a plastic beetle and peered at it. She picked up a grasshopper in her other hand and then another bug. She did not look at her teacher, but Gigi stayed close to make sure Danica was comfortable with the new experience. Danica began to line up the bugs on the table but ignored the playdough and other materials. Gigi sat near Danica and asked, "Can you tell me about the bugs?" Danica began to tell Gigi all about the characteristics of each bug. When she mentioned the bugs' habitats, Gigi said, "I wonder if we could build a home for the bugs with the sticks and playdough." Danica touched the sticks gently and continued talking about the bugs' habitats. Then she picked up the sticks one by one and placed them in between each bug lined up on the table. Danica was very interested in the bugs and sticks all through the makerspace time.

As the time to transition to lunch drew nearer, Gigi knew she would need to help Danica by giving her a warning ahead of time. She told Danica it would soon be time to leave the bugs in their homes and move to the other room for lunch. The warning before the transition helped Danica prepare for the change, and with Gigi's guidance she was able to calmly transition to the next learning experience.

ROLE MODEL

A role model is someone who influences the behavior of those around them. Some teachers may not think of themselves as role models, yet their students regularly imitate their words and actions. Teachers can be good role models of social skills, such as cooperating, communicating effectively, and getting along with others. They model manners when they use courtesy words, such as *please* and *thank you* to the children and other adults in the room. Teachers model how to be kind and help others. Within a makerspace, some children may need help getting started with new and unfamiliar materials. A teacher can model how to use a tool and then give the child the opportunity to test and discover how the tool is used. Think about what you want the children to learn from you. What skills and behaviors can you model? Remember children are watching you and will mimic your words and actions.

QUESTIONER

Asking intentional questions can enhance children's curiosity. Questions can also help teachers gain a greater understanding of children's thought process. In a makerspace, the teacher can expand children's learning by asking questions that require deeper thinking. Questions such as "Can you tell me how you made that?" and "Why did you choose to use those materials?" will show the child that you are interested in his work and will encourage him to engage in a conversation with you.

Questioning styles can either spark or diminish a conversation, depending on how responsive the questions are to young children's interests and play. Mary Hohmann, coauthor of *Educating Young Children* has said, "To expand children's thinking, the questioner will ask questions sparingly. Asking multiple questions takes the control away from the child's conversation. The questioner will relate questions directly to what the child is doing and ask questions about the child's thought process rather than about facts."

Benjamin Bloom and colleagues, noted educators who contributed to the area of cognitive development, created a system to categorize thinking. Using this framework, known as Bloom's Taxonomy, the questioner intentionally asks questions that challenge children to create, evaluate, and analyze. In the next portion of this chapter, we will expand on the topic of intentional questioning.

 # ASKING INTENTIONAL QUESTIONS TO PROMOTE CRITICAL-THINKING SKILLS

In the book *Powerful Interactions*, authors Amy Laura Dombro, Judy Jablon, and Charlotte Stetson write, "Questions have the power to turn children's brains on and get them thinking in new ways."

Acting as "investigative reporters" during makerspace experiences, teachers can discover more about what children are thinking and experiencing. They can use this information to learn more about children's developing skills and how to enhance future makerspace experiences.

Because open-ended questions do not require children to give specific answers, they can promote back-and-forth conversations. Asking open-ended questions helps to support the development of children's cognitive skills by encouraging them to express their thinking and explain their thought processes. The teacher can then use this information to scaffold and enhance children's understanding of the world.

> Miss Callie included open-ended questions in her makerspace experience in a fun way. She pretended to be an investigative reporter and went around the room interviewing her students. She used a small clipboard to record the things the children said and to document their learning.
>
> One morning, when the children had just begun to become engaged in the makerspace, she noticed Juan, a four-year-old, with a clipboard and pencil in his hand. Juan approached a few other children and asked them, "Why did you use those materials?" and "What are you going to do next?" As the other children responded to Juan, he pretended to write what they said on his paper. Juan was imitating Callie and demonstrating his developing social, language, and emerging writing skills.

According to a statement from the Pittsburgh Public Schools Early Childhood Coaches of 2016, "Open-ended questions engage children, stimulate curiosity, inspire creativity, develop language skills, build vocabulary, and cost programs nothing!" The list of possible questions is as endless as are the ideas that will come from the children. Here is an example of a teacher asking intentional, open-ended questions.

> Charlee read the children a story about a bear whose chair had been broken. She asked the children if they wanted to help create a chair strong enough to hold a bear. Oliver was very excited to try. Charlee asked, "What materials do you think you will need to build a chair for the bear?" Oliver smiled widely and looked around at the makerspace materials on the table. He found some cardboard packing pieces and began crafting a chair for the plastic counting bears in the classroom. Charlee observed Oliver working hard to connect the cardboard to a paper tube with masking tape and asked him, "What materials did you use to create the chair?" Oliver proudly described the materials he had chosen. Charlee then asked, "How did you think of that?" and their conversation continued. Soon other children had gathered around to see the chair Oliver had created. "How many bears will it hold?" asked Samantha. Oliver's eyes got big, and he said he did not know as he reached for another plastic bear to stick on the top of his chair. The children excitedly added one bear at a time until the chair Oliver had created toppled over. Oliver frowned and looked at Charlee. "Oh no! What happened?" she asked.
>
> "We wanted to put all the bears on the chair, but it was too many and it broke," Oliver answered.
>
> Charlee responded, "I wonder how you could rebuild the chair to support all the bears."
>
> Oliver looked at the other children and then at the materials on the table. After a long pause, Oliver said, "I am going to use more tape." He went to work, carefully securing the cardboard back to the paper tube with the help of his classmates.

Oliver was motivated to think about the design for his chair because he was interested in solving the problem. His teacher facilitated his experience by asking him open-ended questions to prompt his own critical-thinking and problem-solving skills. Charlee did not try to solve the problem for Oliver or to take over; she simply asked intentional questions and engaged in a thoughtful conversation with him.

Asking intentional, open-ended questions does not always come easily and takes practice. Some teachers have found it is helpful to have a list of possible questions available to prompt their thinking. Consider keeping a list of questions on a card in your pocket or post some sample questions around the room. Having the questions visible can also be helpful to prompt classroom helpers to ask them when they interact with the children. The following list will get you thinking about the types of questions you can ask. Adapt the questions to meet the needs of specific children and situations.

It is important to remember that some children will not respond immediately when they are asked open-ended questions. You may need to think of ways to rephrase the question or may need to simply be persistent, as Charlee does in this example.

> When Charlee first started asking open-ended questions during makerspace experiences, she noticed some children did not answer her at all. She wondered if the children were not ready to answer higher-level thinking questions, but she kept asking the questions and did not give up. As the children in her class got used to these types of questions, they began responding to her more often.

Open-Ended Questions to Ask during Makerspace Experiences

- What are you going to create today?
- How did you think of this idea?
- What materials are you going to use?
- Why did you choose to use those materials?
- What other materials would you like to use?
- What are you planning next?
- How do you think you could change it?

- What else could you add?
- Tell me what you were thinking about.
- I wonder what would happen if . . .
- What do you imagine . . . ?
- Where have you seen that before?
- How could we document that?
- Did that give you any new ideas?
- What could you do next?

- How did you put it together?
- How does it work?
- What do you like best about your creation?
- What do you know about the materials you see or will use?
- How many ways can you . . . ?

Sometimes, children are not familiar with open-ended questions or they simply need more time to think of their answer. A long moment of silence can feel uncomfortable, but avoid the temptation to answer your own questions. Give children time to reflect before they respond. If you find children are not responding after you have paused, try talking about what you see them doing.

> Miss Earnen asked Zach, a young three-year old, "Can you tell me how you made your creation?" Zach did not respond and seemed to be ignoring her as he continued working with the materials. Miss Earnen watched quietly and then made eye contact with Zach, who remained silent.
>
> After a few minutes, Miss Earnen said, "I see you have used some chenille stems and weaved them into the holes on that basket. How did you get the chenille stems to stick together like that?"
>
> Zack answered, "Used this tape." Miss Earnen smiled and continued to describe the details of the child's work.

Remember, with open-ended questions there is not a right or wrong answer. Some children may give you a detailed account of how their creation came to be, and other children will need a bit of encouragement to verbalize their thoughts and ideas. Differences in how children respond may depend on factors such as each child's personality, temperament, and verbal skills. Continue to intentionally ask open-ended questions and give children opportunities to express themselves, demonstrate their understanding, ask for help, and share details about the things they have created. With time, practice, and encouragement, children will begin to give more detailed responses to your questions.

Asking the right questions is part of having rich conversations during a makerspace experience. As you engage children in conversations, base your responses on what a child has said—an approach called *contingent responding*. Contingent responding includes following the child's lead and tuning into what the child has said. Build the conversation by adding related information. This type of responding can extend the conversational loop with additional back-and-forth responses. Contingent responding requires a teacher to pay close attention to what the child is saying or doing, keep the conversation focused on the child, and build on the child's interests. It includes following up on a child's statements by asking for more information or details. Contingent responding is a great way to extend the conversation.

> During a pop-up makerspace, Robin was sitting on the floor with a four-year-old child exploring some plastic cups. He began to stack the cups and said, "I'm building them tall." Robin responded, "I see you are building them tall. How did you think of that?" When the child answered, "It's a tower," Robin followed the lead of the child and responded, "You used the cups to build a tall tower. Have you seen a tower like that before?" The child replied, "Yes, my daddy works at a tower." The conversation between Robin and the child continued based on the back-and-forth exchanges.

Take a few minutes to think about the many ways you can ask intentional, open-ended questions during your makerspace experience.

During a makerspace experience, teachers take on many roles. As we have seen, each of the caps teachers wear during makerspace experiences is vital to creating positive and enriching learning opportunities for young children. With practice, you can become like the cap peddler who balances the many-colored hats without dropping any of them. Be mindful of how you are wearing each of these caps, as all of these roles are important to young children's development. In the next chapter, we explore the phases of a maker.

7

THE PHASES OF A MAKER

In this chapter, we explore the phases that children often go through as they are involved in a makerspace experience. Preschoolers seem almost compelled to explore their immediate environment. They use all their senses to touch, poke, stare at, smell, or carefully listen to the environment and objects around them. We have observed a variety of approaches children display when they first encounter a makerspace. We have also noticed a progression of growth as children become more comfortable exploring, problem solving, and developing new ideas, which we call "the phases of a maker":

- The wonder phase
- The gather phase
- The formulate phase
- The explore phase
- The connect phase
- The apply phase
- The share phase

Some of you may be familiar with a board game called Chutes and Ladders by Hasbro, in which the players spin a spinner and move the number of spaces indicated. A player may land on a space where a ladder advances them quickly to the next level, or in some instances a chute will take the player right back to the beginning of the game. The phases of a maker are much like this game. Children sometimes move through the phases in the order presented, but they may also move through the phases in a different sequence. We like to think of it as children following different paths on their makerspace journeys. Younger children often stay in the explore phase longer than older children. With more experience in a makerspace, children spend more time in the apply phase. Teachers can support children by recognizing the phase a child is in. Let's take a look at the phases in more detail.

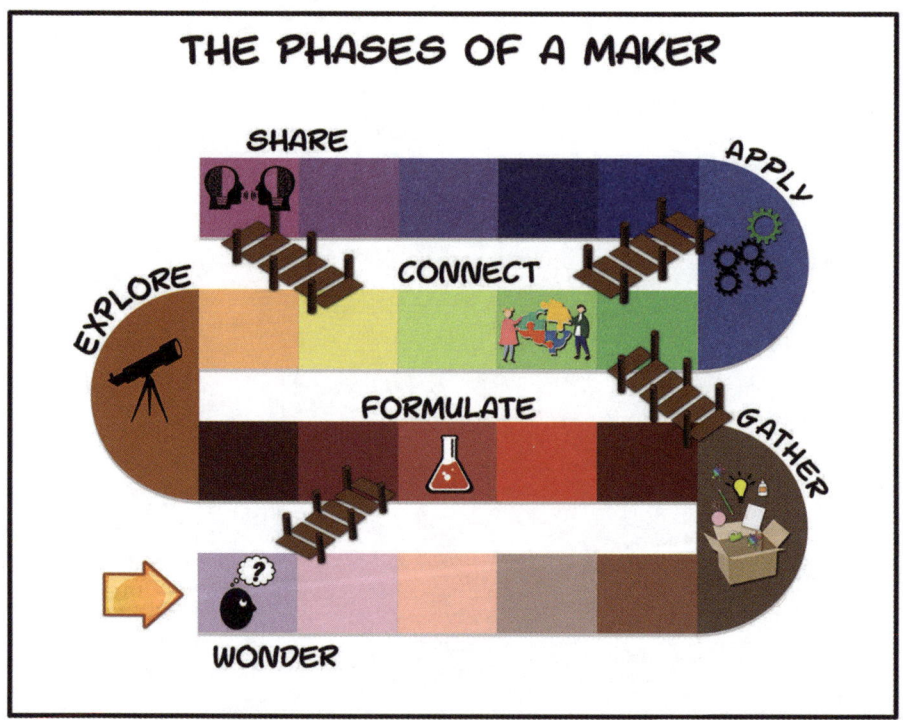

⚙⚙ THE WONDER PHASE ⚙⚙

Wonder is an emotion similar to the surprise that a person feels when encountering something unexpected or unfamiliar. Wonder is often linked with curiosity and sparks exploration. Children experiencing a makerspace for the first time may be a bit timid and may feel reluctant to touch the materials and tools. Some children will wait and observe the teacher or peers from a distance before engaging with any of the materials. Children may wonder what to do and how to use the tools and materials. They may watch with wonder as other children interact with materials. Being able to observe others provides these children with time to evaluate and determine how they will interact with the items in the space. Some children, especially if they are highly curious, move through the wonder stage without hesitancy and immediately begin examining materials, testing tools, and gathering items of interest.

Remember that children will approach makerspace experiences differently. We discovered that younger children or those who were participating in makerspace for the first time often approach the materials differently than older children or those who had previously been exposed to makerspace experiences. Younger children often spend more time investigating materials and usually work independently. One way to promote collaborative learning experiences is to engage children in a variety of small design challenges.

In Callie's class at Handprints in the Highlands, the three-year-old children spent most of their time working alone. She noticed that, occasionally, some of the children would watch and copy one another, but they rarely collaborated on their designs. Callie set a goal to develop opportunities that would encourage the children to work together.

The next day, in the makerspace interest center, Callie placed the children into small groups for a design challenge. She noticed that even when she was intentionally trying to encourage the children to work together, many of the younger children still worked independently. Callie was not discouraged and decided to take a more active role in the process. She joined a small group of three young boys. She noticed that the boys did share ideas with each other;

however, they needed additional prompting and support to come up with a collaborative design. Callie modeled how to collaborate. Over time, the children in Callie's class began teaming up more often.

SUGGESTED TEACHER ACTIONS DURING THE WONDER PHASE

- Notice children's sense of wonder and how they are responding to the makerspace.
- Pay attention to children's level of engagement, and take note of which materials and tools they are drawn to.
- Ask children, "What are you wondering about?" and "What looks interesting to you?"
- Ask children, "What are you thinking of creating?" and "What do you think you could make with these materials and tools?"
- Comment on children's interests: "It looks like you are interested in . . ."

THE GATHER PHASE

Gathering has a two-fold meaning during this phase. Children are gathering information as they observe, touch, and manipulate materials. Preschoolers begin asking questions and seeking answers about the makerspace materials and tools. They are also physically gathering items. Their senses take it all in during this stage. You can almost see the gears turning as a child looks inside an old computer at the wires, nuts, and bolts and wonders how to take it all apart. Each item they touch has the potential of being used in a different way, and they gather items that are of interest to them.

SUGGESTED TEACHER ACTIONS DURING THE GATHER PHASE

- After noticing what children are drawn to, think about what materials you could add. What additional items would support children's interests and development in future makerspace

experiences? Remember that adding and rotating materials will keep children intrigued in the makerspace.

- Ask children, "What else looks interesting?" "What are you thinking about making?" and "What will you need for your creation?"
- Comment on the materials that children have gathered. "I can't wait to see what you will be doing with the string, tin foil, and cardboard tube."

⚙⚙ THE FORMULATE PHASE ⚙⚙

While children are gathering information and materials, they begin to formulate ideas about how they might use the items. A multitude of ideas may be percolating in a child's mind as she moves about the makerspace. During this phase, ideas are fluid. The next item a child sees or touches may change the direction of her thought process. Ideas and plans begin to take shape and prototypes begin to become more concrete in her mind. These ideas and plans spur the curious child to bring her thoughts to life.

SUGGESTED TEACHER ACTIONS
DURING THE FORMULATE PHASE

- As you observe the children, think about ways to enhance future makerspace experiences that align with your program's philosophy, curriculum, and lessons. Consider ways that you can individualize learning experiences and set up opportunities that will support the desired outcomes.
- Ask children, "Would you like to draw out your plan?" and "What steps will you need to take to make your creation?"
- Ask children, "Can you tell me about your plan?" and "What are you planning on doing first?"
- Comment on the plans the children have made: "I like how you have drawn pictures of the materials you will need for your creation."

⚙ THE EXPLORE PHASE ⚙

Children who explore makerspace materials often discover something they did not know before or something other than what they expected. Children actively manipulate maker materials while examining objects, making observations, and formulating ideas. They are figuring out components and constructing their own understanding of the materials. Exploring items of interest also leads to connections. Do you remember the story we shared earlier about the child who was fascinated with exploring tape? Children often need to explore materials thoroughly before they are ready to create with them. Give children the time and space to explore the materials and tools.

SUGGESTED TEACHER ACTIONS
DURING THE EXPLORE PHASE

- Encourage children's independence and autonomy as they investigate materials and develop hypotheses on how to use them.
- Encourage children to interact with new materials and to try unfamiliar tools.
- Ask children, "How do you think this works?" and "What would happen if . . ."
- Comment on children's explorations: "I noticed that you are trying out different ways to use the screwdriver." "I can see that you are discovering a variety of ways to use the . . ."

⚙ THE CONNECT PHASE ⚙

You may have heard the expression "connect the dots," which refers to the ability to associate one idea with another and discover a bigger picture. The connect phase occurs when a child connects the dots after gathering information, formulating ideas, and exploring possibilities. Ellen Galinsky, author of *Mind in the Making* has said, "When children are able to make connections that are unusual or that go against the norm, they have the basis for true creative thinking."

As children observe their peers with similar interests or those who have a better understanding of how something works, they often mirror that interest to enhance their own knowledge. Ellen Galinsky further states, "Teachers can promote making connections by giving children feedback on their thinking. . . Children make connections as they try out different ideas. Sometimes these ideas do not work out as planned, and teachers can encourage children to keep trying out other ideas. Teachers can help children connect why the idea did not work out as planned and how to apply what they learned and move forward."

SUGGESTED TEACHER ACTIONS DURING THE CONNECT PHASE

- Help children find connections related to what worked and what did not work.
- Ask questions to promote higher-level thinking: "How did you solve the problem?" "Why do you think it happened that way?" and "What could we do differently next time?"
- Support children in investigating materials, connecting concepts, and testing hypotheses.
- Comment on how children are using their thinking skills: "I noticed you tried three different strategies to solve the problem. Great problem solving!"

⚙⚙⚙ THE APPLY PHASE ⚙⚙⚙

As children learn new information about materials and tools in the makerspace, they become engaged in seeking solutions and testing new ideas. They begin applying knowledge from one experience to the next. Children propose explanations and compare their own thinking with that of their peers. They often become quite focused as they build, create, and explore. The information they have gathered and formulated into a plan comes to life, and they are excited to see the results.

SUGGESTED TEACHER ACTIONS DURING THE APPLY PHASE

- Pay attention to how children have applied their knowledge and experience during the makerspace experience.
- Acknowledge children's processes and what they have learned and created.
- Ask intentional questions to prompt the thought process and promote critical thinking. Ask children, "How did you come up with your design?" and "Why did you use these specific materials and tools?"
- Comment on how children applied their knowledge and skills during the process: "The last time you built a bridge, you discovered that you need to support the middle. I see that you used that information on this bridge. Great thinking!"

⚙️⚙️ THE SHARE PHASE ⚙️⚙️

Do you remember show-and-tell events when you were in elementary school? More than likely, you brought a special object to school and showed your classmates how it worked or what made it unique. You probably felt great excitement as you shared your item. Likewise, children will be excited to share their knowledge, creations, and discoveries with others during a makerspace experience. As children complete a task or successfully build a structure, they will often seek their teacher or a friend and describe what they did and what they discovered.

As children develop and mature, their play and social interactions change. This is true during makerspace experiences as well. In classrooms where four- and five-year-old children are engaging in a makerspace, we usually see more collaboration and sharing of ideas. What we observe will vary based on the individual children in the group—their temperaments and personalities—but children often plan and design together more frequently with time and experience. The following is an example of how three children in a prekindergarten classroom designed a habitat for a turtle together.

> The children had been learning about different animal habitats. A small group of three children decided they wanted to create a habitat for a turtle. The children discussed what could go into the habitat. They decided the turtle needed a nice house that included a TV and a comfortable place to relax. The children began making the different items for the turtle's home. Together they constructed a building that included a room for a TV. They designed a throw pillow so that the turtle could relax after swimming all day. These children had experience working together, and this led to a natural collaboration as they created the habitat.

SUGGESTED TEACHER ACTIONS
DURING THE SHARE PHASE

- Engage with the children in the makerspace as they test hypotheses and share their results.
- Support children when things do not go as planned, and have them share what they did and what they could try next.

- Take pictures to share and document progress. Sharing photos of creations made in the makerspace are great ways to include families, administrators, and other key stakeholders.
- Ask children, "Can you share with me how you made your creation?" and "What was your favorite part of the makerspace experience?"
- Comment on what children share: "I love how you combined the different materials to create your robot." "You were very creative in how you made your bridge so that it could hold the weight of the bears."

The phases of a maker are developed through firsthand experience, observation, and feedback. Awareness of these phases will better prepare you to support and facilitate children's explorations as they navigate a makerspace. You may observe other phases that are specific to the children you teach. That is the beauty of a makerspace—it is not a cookie-cutter process. We invite you to be intentional in planning and to find joy with the children in makerspace experiences.

BECOME THE MAKER CHAMPION

Think about the different approaches to creating and using a makerspace in your classroom we have offered. Teachers play a vital role in the exciting discovery of making. We hope the information we have shared eases the learning curve as you begin your journey as a maker in a makerspace and inspires you to confidently allow children the opportunity to take part in the exciting world of makerspaces. We want your makerspaces to succeed, to expand the maker community, and to grow the maker movement. To those ends, we offer the following list of online resources.

Makerspace Online Resources

Doorley, Rachelle. 2020. The Tinker Lab: A Hands-On Guide for Little Inventors. https://tinkerlab.com/

Exploratorium. 2020. Learning Dimensions of Making and Tinkering: A professional development tool for educators. https://www.exploratorium.edu/tinkering/our-work/learning-dimensions-making-and-tinkering

Instructables. 2020. "Yours for the Making." 2020. Instructables. http://www.instructables.com/

Makerspaces.com. 2014. "Ultimate Makerspace Guide" Makerspaces.com. https://www.makerspaces.com/makerspace-guide-school-and-library/

Rendina, Diana. 2020. "Makerspace Resources." Renovated Learning. http://www.renovatedlearning.com/makerspace-resources/

Seymour, Gina. 2020. "8 Ways to Build a More Inclusive Makerspace." Ideas & Inspiration. https://ideas.demco.com/blog/8-ways-build-more-inclusive-makerspace/

We hope you will experience the satisfaction of observing children fully participating in the makerspaces you offer. Watch as children discover new ideas and let their natural innovation guide them. We have discovered the joy of sharing the makerspace ideas with others in our community and have seen the excitement grow. We encourage you to share your experiences with coworkers, families, and your community. Invite others into your makerspace to experience the magic of discovery, problem solving, and creativity. We challenge you to become a maker champion and promote the maker movement in early childhood!

TEN LESSONS LEARNED: TIPS FROM EXPERIENCED MAKERSPACE TEACHERS

Lesson 1: It is a process. The more teachers and children participate in makerspace experiences, the more comfortable they will become. Teachers and children benefit from ongoing makerspace experiences over time. Learning and growing within a makerspace experience does take time and is a process, so be willing to be patient and stick with it.

Lesson 2: It takes a team and a community. Some teachers may feel nervous when they first begin providing makerspace experiences to young children. Working in teams and having extra support in the classroom during makerspace experiences helps boost teachers' confidence.

Lesson 3: It takes a plan. Before their first makerspace experience, teachers need time to plan together to discuss how they will set up the space and to determine the roles that each adult will take during the makerspace experience. Determine which areas will have tools and materials that need extra supervision, and plan accordingly. Discuss ways that adults can enhance the makerspace experience by asking children intentional, open-ended questions and taking note of what the children are interested in.

Lesson 4: It takes follow-up. After each makerspace experience, meet with your coteachers and discuss the experience. What were the preferred materials and learning experiences? How did the children interact with the materials and tools? What additional materials or tools could you add to the next makerspace experience? For example, remember the child who needed a baby screwdriver for the video camera? The teachers would make a reminder to bring a baby screwdriver to the next makerspace experience, so that child feels that his suggestion was heard and his ideas were valued.

Lesson 5: It takes trial and error. We asked some of the teachers who tried makerspaces in their classrooms about how the experience changed over time. Charlee said, "One of the first times I had a makerspace, I put out way too many materials. I had to think about what materials would pair best together and be intentional about what to put out."

Lesson 6: It takes being intentional. It is better to be intentional and to focus on including materials that will spark children's curiosity and creativity. For example, Ms. Takisha realized that if she put out power tools in one area, that area would need her full attention. In the future, she needed to ensure that the children could use the rest of the materials and tools she included more independently. She also realized that a successful makerspace experience did not need to include all of the items at once.

Lesson 7: It includes familiar and unfamiliar items. As you introduce a makerspace to children, you may find that they are drawn to one type of material. We noticed that children will typically first approach either the materials they are familiar with or the materials that are new and unfamiliar to them. It is important to have both types of materials. Some children are drawn to tools that they may have seen before but have not used. They will often approach these items with curiosity and excitement, wanting to discover how each tool works. Other groups of children will be drawn to the more familiar materials, such as tape, cardboard, and craft sticks. These children are motivated by the desire to explore materials they recognize.

Lesson 8: It includes multiples of children's favorites. We asked several teachers about the type of materials that were a favorite for their groups of children. One teacher enthusiastically responded, "They loved tape!" She told us that tape was an essential material for almost every makerspace in her classroom. She shared that the children used tape on creations such as bridges made of craft sticks and chairs made from cardboard and tubes. For her, tape was in such high demand that she invested in rolls of tape by the dozen. She shared, "Once each child had their own roll of tape, no one had to wait for a turn, and every child was able to create what was on their mind as soon as they thought of it." The essential or favorite material may vary for your group of children. It takes time, observation, and reflection to discover what will inspire them.

Lesson 9: It includes ample time and space. When reflecting on makerspace experiences in early childhood classrooms, all the teachers we talked with said they would recommend it for others. Miss Nicole, an assistant teacher in a four-year-old class, said, "It tapped into their creativity and imagination; it is vital that they experience these things at this age." When observing children who are engaged in a makerspace, it is easy to see their creativity, imagination, and problem solving in action. Children are energized by the opportunity to explore independently and apply their ideas as they become deeply involved in their work. They need ample time and space to immerse themselves in making and creating.

Lesson 10: It includes teachers scaffolding children's learning. Teachers shared the importance of having meaningful conversations with the children during makerspace experiences. They felt they were able to scaffold learning when they asked intentional, open-ended questions, which prompted the children to elaborate on their ideas. There were many ah-ha moments of self-discovery during these conversations.

APPENDICES

APPENDIX A: MAKERSPACE REFLECTION QUESTIONNAIRE

Completing this questionnaire will guide you and your team in the process of thinking about and planning for makerspace experiences. This form may be used by an individual teacher, a small teaching team, or a designated program team to assist in the makerspace planning process.

WHAT

- What do we want to do? Define your dream makerspace.
- What are the benefits of creating a makerspace?

WHY

- Why are we interested in setting up a makerspace?
- What big ideas are we hoping to achieve?
- What goals would we like to accomplish?

WHO

- Who is it for? Which children will have makerspace experiences?
- How would a makerspace benefit the children in our program?

WHERE AND WHEN

- What spaces could we use? Could we set up the makerspace in a classroom interest center or in a separate room? If not, would we be able to bring the materials into the classroom as needed?
- What are the best days and times for the children to have makerspace experiences, if a makerspace is not a permanent classroom interest center?
- How often will makerspace experiences be available?

SAFETY

- Will we need additional supervision/adult facilitation during makerspace experiences?
- Who could we ask to provide additional support?
- What tools and materials within the makerspace will need extra safety guidance?

MATERIALS

- What materials and tools do we currently have that could be used in a makerspace?
- What additional materials could we add that would be appropriate and culturally responsive to the children in our program?

STORAGE

- What storage containers do we have that we could utilize for makerspace materials and tools?
- What storage containers will we need to purchase or have donated?
- Where will the makerspace materials and tools be stored?

PROGRAM PHILOSOPHY

- What aspects of a makerspace match our program's philosophy?
- What current program policies and procedures do we need to consider when setting up the makerspace?
- What ways can we meet our program's learning objectives during makerspace experiences?

MEETING CHILDREN'S INDIVIDUAL NEEDS

- How can we ensure the makerspace is accessible to all the children?
- What individual accommodations will we need to make for individual children?

- What are the current interests and developmental levels of the children who will participate?
- What materials can we bring in that will be culturally relevant to the children?
- What developmental needs do the children in our group currently have that could be enhanced within a makerspace?

INVOLVING FAMILIES

- What is the best way to introduce makerspace to families?
- How do we think families will respond?
- How could we involve families?

FUNDING

- What funds could we utilize? For example, could we apply for grant funds? Could we take donations?
- How much will the makerspace cost to set up and maintain?
- Where can we obtain free or low-cost materials and tools?

OTHER

- What other things do we need to consider as we set up a makerspace?
- Who will train staff on implementing a makerspace experience?
- How will we evaluate the makerspace experience?

APPENDIX B: MAKERSPACE FAMILY QUESTIONNAIRE

Young children are interested in many different things. This questionnaire is designed to help us learn more about your child's interests and family. We are setting up makerspaces in our program. Makerspaces are spaces for children to engage in exploring materials and creating something they imagine. With the information from this questionnaire, we can enrich the makerspace experience for your child.

Please tell us about your CHILD by answering the following questions.

1. What activities outside your home is your child most interested or involved in? (e.g., music, dance, outdoor sports, swimming)
2. What activities in the home is your child most interested or involved in? (e.g., building with Legos/blocks, drawing, pretend play, simple games)
3. What types of books is your child most interested in? (e.g., animals, planes, trains, automobiles, fairy tales)
4. What new things has your child learned recently? (e.g., somersault, pedal a bike, draw a person with a body, recall parts of a story)
5. If your child helps around the home, how do they help? (e.g., set the table, fold laundry, pick up toys, clean up spills)
6. How does your child typically interact with other children? (e.g., plays alone, watches but does not interact, plays alongside, cooperative play)
7. How does your child typically respond to new situations and challenges? (e.g., anxious, unsure, fearful, excited, confident, adventurous)

Families play an essential role in every aspect of the developing child's life. We would like to know more about your rich and interesting cultural heritage. We also want to learn more about how families would like to help with our program's makerspace experiences.

Please tell us about your FAMILY by answering the following questions.

1. What languages are spoken in your home?
2. What types of jobs do family members have?
3. What activities does your child enjoy doing as a family? (e.g., travel, play games, hiking, hobbies)

4. What people and/or pets are important to your child? (e.g., siblings, grand-parents, aunts and uncles, close friend)
5. How does your family celebrate important events? (e.g., birthdays, holidays, cultural celebrations)
6. Do you have some things that reflect your culture and background that you are willing to show or share with us in the classroom? (e.g., talents, hobbies, pictures, tools, stories) If so, please list.
7. Do you have materials you are willing to donate to the makerspace in the classroom that are related to your child's heritage? If so, please list.
8. What other interests would you like us to know about your child and family?

We value the information you have provided and are excited for your child to experience "making" in our program's makerspace!

APPENDIX C: DRAFTING THE PLAN: PROGRAM PLANNING GUIDE

Use the following questions to draft a plan for your makerspace.

WHERE?

- Where will your makerspace be located?
- What steps do you need to take to prepare your space?

WHEN?

When will children have opportunities to engage in the makerspace? daily, once a week? Plan out your schedule.

WHAT DO YOU HAVE?

What materials, tools, and storage do you currently have that you could use in your makerspace? See the materials and tools list on pages 36–37.

WHAT DO YOU NEED?

What materials, tools, and storage do you want to add to your makerspace? See the materials and tools list on pages 36–37 for ideas.

Example 1: Learn and Grow Child Care (Tinker Trays)

WHERE?

- Where will your makerspace be located? On tables in the classroom
- What steps do you need to take to prepare your space?

- Materials will be placed on trays set on tables
- Materials will be stored in rolling storage carts
- Need to organize materials on carts and tray

WHEN?

When will children have opportunities to engage in the makerspace? Plan out your schedule.

- Makerspace will be offered weekly on Tuesdays and will be planned into the daily schedule
- Plan with coteacher which specific opportunities and challenges to offer that will support the needs of children

WHAT DO YOU HAVE?

What materials, tools, and storage do you currently have that you could use in your makerspace?

- Tables, trays
- Tools, woodworking materials, donated items such as electronics
- Scissors, tape, pencils, crayons, markers
- Small clipboards
- Creative-arts materials

WHAT DO YOU NEED?

What materials, tools, and storage do you want to add to your makerspace?

- Three rolling storage carts
- Natural materials
- Upcycled and recycled materials
- Tools and woodworking materials
- Electronics
- Books to be used as prompts for ideas

Example 2: Handprints in the Highlands (Interest Center)

WHERE?

- Where will your makerspace be located? Located as interest center in the classroom
- What steps do you need to take to prepare your space?
    - Need to rearrange the classroom to set up makerspace interest center
    - Need to bring in rolling shelves
    - Need to add space between tables
    - Need to add materials and tools

WHEN?

When will children have opportunities to engage in the makerspace? Plan out your schedule.

- The makerspace will be a daily interest-center choice during free-choice time.
- Add makerspace time into daily schedule (during choice time and some transitions)
- Weekly: plan activities, questions, and challenges with coteacher that align with monthly theme

WHAT DO YOU HAVE?

What materials, tools, and storage do you currently have that you could use in your makerspace?

- Interest boxes with open-ended materials
- One cart and shelves, tables
- Storage closet
- Some recycled materials
- Natural materials

WHAT DO YOU NEED?

What materials, tools, and storage do you want to add to your makerspace?

- Two more carts/shelves to store items
- Open-ended creative art materials
- Tools and woodworking materials
- Electronics
- Safety goggles

Example 3: Sunny Days Preschool (Designated Room)

WHERE?

- Where will your makerspace be located? Located in empty classroom
- What steps do you need to take to prepare your space?
    - Need to rearrange the furniture
    - Need to remove nonessential materials
    - Need to bring in rolling carts and permanent storage closet for maker-space materials

WHEN?

When will children have opportunities to engage in the makerspace? Plan out your schedule.

- Makerspace offered weekly for each preschool classroom and by special request
- Plan schedule for each classroom's makerspace day and times
- Teaching teams will work together to create design challenges based on the needs of the children

WHAT DO YOU HAVE?

What materials, tools, and storage do you currently have that you could use in your makerspace?

- Available classroom
- Sink
- Shelving
- Tools and building materials
- Donated electronics
- Smart tablet
- Green screen

WHAT DO YOU NEED?

What materials, tools, and storage do you want to add to your makerspace?

- Storage carts
- Rug
- Recycled and upcycled items
- Books to use as prompts
- Movie app or software to use with green screen to create children's movie productions

APPENDIX D: LETTERS TO REQUEST DONATIONS

LETTER TO FAMILIES

Dear Families,

Our classroom is starting something new and exciting called a makerspace. It is an invitation for young children to boldly explore materials and to create something only they can imagine, either independently or collaboratively. Children are provided resources and teacher guidance throughout the process. A makerspace is designed to encourage children to practice real-world problem solving, in an engaging, challenging way.

We feel it is important for children to have experiences that represent different cultures and diverse groups. This can be accomplished by including materials, shared stories, and talents from family members. Do you have items that reflect your culture and background that you are willing to show or share with us in the classroom (e.g., talents, hobbies, photos, tools, stories)? Do you have materials you are willing to donate to the makerspace in our classroom that reflect your child's heritage?

We gladly accept your contribution for creating diverse makerspace experiences for the children.

Examples of items to donate:

Woodworking tools, mesh strainer, chopsticks, whisk, hand grinder, stone bowl and pestle, lemon squeezer, potato masher, tortilla press, sewing tools, grinding stone, mauls, shaping tools, levers, clamps, leather, music instruments, etc.

Please note some items are unsafe or not approved by Child Care licensing. We are unable to accept items such as toilet paper rolls, used egg cartons, products bearing the CL (caution label), etc. If you have a question about items for donation, please contact your child's classroom teacher.

A donation container will be located outside of the classroom in the_____ (identify location).

Thank you for contributing to our makerspace!

LETTER TO COMMUNITY BUSINESSES

[Date]

[Center or Program]

[Address]

[City, State Zip code]

Dear Sir or Madam [or business name]:

I am writing on behalf of [center or program name], which is developing a makerspace in our early childhood classroom. A makerspace is an area where young children boldly explore materials and create something only they can imagine, either independently or collaboratively. Materials used during a makerspace experience include upcycled items, old electronics, creative art supplies, natural materials, woodworking materials, tools and many items that provide extended learning opportunities for children. The staff at [center or program name] are excited to provide young children with hands-on experiences using a variety of makerspace materials.

We are asking for your generous donation of _____[specific or general items] that can be used in our makerspace. Items donated will be assessed for safety before being placed in the makerspace area. We will gladly pick up donated items, or they can be dropped off at our location.

We value our local businesses and look forward to forging community connections with your company.

Sincerely,

[Your name]

[Title- if applicable]

REFERENCES AND RECOMMENDED READINGS

Association of American Colleges and Universities. 2018. *Fulfilling the American Dream: Liberal Education and the Future of Work.* Washington, DC: Association of American Colleges and Universities. https://www.aacu.org/sites/default/files/files/LEAP/2018EmployerResearchReport.pdf

Batra, Sunil. 2013. "The Psychosocial Development of Children: Implications for Education and Society—Erik Erikson in Context." *Contemporary Education Dialogue* 10(2): 249–278.

Bloom, Benjamin, et al. 1956. *Taxonomy of Educational Objectives: The Classification of Educational Goals*. New York: Longmans, Green, and Company.

Carey, Barbara, Megan Hernberg, Tanya Hobbs, and Cathy Paul. 2014. "The Maker Movement." *Thinkers and Tinkers*. https://hernbergm.wixsite.com/maker-movement

Center on the Social and Emotional Foundations for Early Learning. 2021. "Resources: Practical Strategies for Teachers/Caregivers." *Center on the Social and Emotional Foundations for Early Learning*. http://csefel.vanderbilt.edu/resources/strategies.html

Compton, Michelle, and Robin Thompson. 2018. *Story Making: The Maker Movement Approach to Literacy for Early Learners*. St. Paul, MN: Redleaf.

Cropley, Arthur. 2006. "In Praise of Convergent Thinking." *Creativity Research Journal* 18(3): 391–404.

Daly, Lisa, and Miriam Beloglovsky. 2014. *Loose Parts: Inspiring Play in Young Children*. St. Paul, MN: Redleaf.

DeViney, Jessica, et al. 2010. *Inspiring Spaces for Young Children*. Lewisville, NC: Gryphon House.

Dombro, Amy Laura, Judy Jablon, and Charlotte Stetson. 2011. *Powerful Interactions: How to Connect with Children to Extend Their Learning*. Washington, DC: The National Association for the Education of Young Children.

Dougherty, Dale. 2012. "The Maker Movement." *Innovations* 7(3): 11–14. https://www.mitpressjournals.org/doi/pdf/10.1162/INOV_a_00135

Englehart, Deirdre, et al. 2016. *STEM Play: Integrating Inquiry into Learning Centers*. Lewisville, NC: Gryphon House.

Erickson, Erik. 1950/1963. *Childhood and Society*. 2nd edition. New York: Norton.

Gabrielson, Curt. 2015. *Tinkering: Kids Learn by Making Stuff*. Sebastopol, CA: Make Community.

Galinsky, Ellen. 2010. *Mind in the Making: The Seven Essential Life Skills Every Child Needs*. New York: HarperStudio.

Gregory, Kara, An Sook Kim, and Alice Whiren. 2003. "The Effect of Verbal Scaffolding on the Complexity of Preschool Children's Block Constructions." In *Play and Educational Theory and Practice.* Westport, CT: Praeger.

Hendrick, Joanne, Patricia Weissman, and Judith Kaminsky. 1998. *The Whole Child: A Care Giver's Guide to the First Five Years.* Englewood Cliffs, NV: Prentice Hall.

Heroman, Cate. 2016. *Making and Tinkering With STEM: Solving Design Challenges with Young Children.* Washington, DC: NAEYC.

Hohmann, Mary, and David Weikart. 2002. *Educating Young Children.* 2nd edition. Ypsilanti, MI: HighScope.

Hughes, Fergus. 2010. *Children, Play, and Development.* 4th edition. Thousand Oaks, CA: SAGE.

Hughes, Janette. 2018. "Can These Spaces Help Kids Be More Creative?" CNN. https://www.cnn.com/2017/09/18/health/kids-makerspaces/index.html

Kaplan Early Learning Company. 2021. "Setting Up Your Preschool Learning Centers." *Insights and Inspirations.* Kaplan Early Learning Company. https://www.kaplanco.com/ii/preschool-learning-centers

Makerspaces.com. n.d. "What Is a Makerspace?" Makerspaces.com. https://www.makerspaces.com/what-is-a-makerspace/

Martinez, Sylvia L., and Gary Stager. 2013. *Invent to Learn: Making, Tinkering, and Engineering in the Classroom.* Torrance, CA: Constructing Modern Knowledge Press.

McDougal, Clint. 2021. "What Influence Does Culture Have on a Student's School Success? Cultural Responsiveness." In *Cultural and Linguistic Differences: What Teachers Should Know.* Nashville, TN: IRIS Center Peabody College Vanderbilt University. https://iris.peabody.vanderbilt.edu/module/clde/cresource/q1/p02/#:~:text=Cultural%20competence%20refers%20to%20an,while%20respecting%20those%20of%20others

Miels, Jill. 2008. "The Seven Faces of the Early Childhood Educator." *Early Childhood News* http://www.earlychildhoodnews.com/earlychildhood/article_view.aspx?ArticleID=171

Murphy, Lisa. 2019. *On Being Child Centered*. St. Paul, MN: Redleaf.

National Association for the Education of Young Children. 2009. "How Do Early Childhood Education Programs Meet the Challenge of Engaging Families in Their Children's Early Learning and Development?" *Principles of Effective Family Engagement*. https://www.naeyc.org/resources/topics/family-engagement/principles

Nemeth, Karen, and Pam Brillante. 2018. "Including All Children in Making and Tinkering." *Teaching Young Children* 11(2).

Norman, Kim. 2015. *If It's Snowy and You Know It, Clap Your Paws!* New York: Sterling Children's Books.

Pepler, Debra, and Hildy Ross. 1981. "The Effects of Play on Convergent and Divergent Problem Solving." *Journal of the Society for Research in Child Development*. 52(4): 1202–1210.

Piers, Maria W., ed. 1972. *Play and Development: A Symposium with Contributions by Jean Piaget, Peter H. Wolff, Rene A. Spitz, Konrad Lorenz, Lois Barclay Murphy, and Erik H. Erikson*. New York: W. W. Norton and Company.

Pittsburgh Public Schools Early Childhood Coaches of 2016. 2020. "Message in a Backpack: Spark Creative Thinking with Open-Ended Questions." *Teaching Young Children* 13(4). https://www.naeyc.org/resources/pubs/tyc/apr2020/message-backpack-spark-creative-thinking

Rogoff, Barbara. 2003. *The Cultural Nature of Human Development*. New York: Oxford University Press.

Saracho, Olivia. 2002. "Young Children's Creativity and Pretend Play." *Early Child Development and Care* 172(5): 431–438.

Slobodkina, Esphyr. 1987. *Caps for Sale: A Tale of a Peddler, Some Monkeys, and Their Monkey Business*. New York: HarperCollins.

Strasser, Janis, and Lisa Bresson. 2015. "Moving Beyond Who, What, When, Where, and Why: Using Bloom's Taxonomy Questioning to Extend Preschoolers' Thinking." *Teaching Young Children* 9(1). https://www.naeyc.org/resources/pubs/tyc/oct2015/using-blooms-taxonomy-questioning

Thomas, AnnMarie. 2014. *Making Makers: Kids, Tools, and the Future of Innovation.* Sebastopol, CA: MakerMedia.

Thompson, Robin, and Michelle Compton. 2019. "Start Story Making to Join the Maker Movement." *Teaching Young Children* 12(3).

Van Hoorn, Judith, Patricia Nourot, Barbara Scales, and Keith Alward. 1999. *Play at the Center of the Curriculum.* 2nd edition. Upper Saddle River, NJ: Merrill.

INDEX